Entrepreneurship
How to Become a Successful Entrepreneur with Creative Mindset

Leslie K Henley

© Copyright 2020 by - All rights reserved.

This document is geared towards providing exact and reliable information in regards to the topic and issue covered. The publication is sold with the idea that the publisher is not required to render accounting, officially permitted, or otherwise, qualified services. If advice is necessary, legal or professional, a practiced individual in the profession should be ordered. From a Declaration of Principles which was accepted and approved equally by a Committee of the American Bar Association and a Committee of Publishers and Associations. In no way is it legal to reproduce, duplicate, or transmit any part of this document in either electronic means or in printed format. Recording of this publication is strictly prohibited and any storage of this document is not allowed unless with written permission from the publisher. All rights reserved.

The information provided herein is stated to be truthful and consistent, in that any liability, in terms of inattention or otherwise, by any usage or abuse of any policies, processes, or directions contained within is the solitary and utter responsibility of the recipient reader. Under no circumstances will any legal responsibility or blame be held against the publisher for any reparation, damages, or monetary loss due to the information herein, either directly or indirectly. Respective authors own all copyrights not held by the publisher. The information herein is offered for informational purposes solely, and is universal as so. The presentation of the information is without contract or any type of guarantee assurance. The trademarks that are used are without any consent, and the publication of the trademark is without permission or backing by the trademark owner. All trademarks and brands within this book are for clarifying purposes only and are the owned by the owners themselves, not affiliated with this document.

Contents

Introduction 4

Chapter 1: Understanding entrepreneurship 7

    1.1 Top Qualities of a Successful Entrepreneur 12

    1.2 The role of creativity in entrepreneurship 20

    1.3 How to Become an Entrepreneur 26

    1.4 Types of Entrepreneurs: Understanding the Unique Differences 32

Chapter 2: 30 Ways to Become a More Successful Entrepreneur 46

    2.1 Entrepreneurial Mindset: 5 Characteristics to Cultivate 49

    2.2 Entrepreneurial Traits for Career Success 54

    2.3 Characteristics of an Entrepreneur 59

Chapter 3: Powerful Ways for Entrepreneurs to Be More Creative 66

    3.1 Role and Importance of Entrepreneurship 72

    3.2 Why Creativity is so Crucial for Entrepreneurs? 77

Chapter 4: 7 Powerful Secrets of Thinking like an Entrepreneure 85

    4.1 12 Characteristics of the World's Most Successful Entrepreneurs 86

Conclusion 89

References 90

Introduction

Entrepreneurship is the act of founding a company or corporation to make a profit while creating and scaling it.

But that one is a little restrictive as a fundamental concept of entrepreneurship. Also, the more modern concept of entrepreneurship is about changing the world by solving big issues like creating social change or creating a revolutionary product that questions the status quo on how we live our lives every day.

What the concept of entrepreneurship does not tell you is that what people do to take their careers and dreams into their hands and lead them in the direction they want is entrepreneurship.

It is about, on your own terms, creating a life. And no managers. No scheduling constraints. And nobody holds you back. The first step can be taken by entrepreneurs in making the world a better place, including themselves and everybody in it.

An entrepreneur is a person who creates a company with the intention of making a profit.

This definition of an entrepreneur can be a little unclear, For good reason, though. An entrepreneur can be an individual who sets up or just starts out as a freelancer with their first online shop on the side.

The reason why, though some disagree, they're called entrepreneurs is that where you start out isn't always where you'll end up.

An entrepreneur is someone who begins a side hustle that can ultimately create employees with a full-time, profitable company. The same thing with a freelancer. You suit the concept of the entrepreneur if your entrepreneurial mentality is based on building a successful business.

But the importance of the entrepreneur requires much more than being a producer of a company or work.

Any of the world's most powerful transformers are entrepreneurs. Entrepreneurs envision the future differently, from Elon Musk sending people to Mars to Bill Gates and Steve Jobs making computers part of every household.

And the concept of entrepreneur hardly ever speaks of the immense influence these thought leaders have on the planet.

What Is Entrepreneurship Meaning?

An entrepreneur who takes steps to make a difference in the world is interested in the sense of entrepreneurship. They all share one thing in common: action, whether start-up founders tackle an issue that many struggles with every day, put people together in a way that no one has before, or create something innovative that advances society.

This isn't some notion trapped in your mind. Entrepreneurs take the definition and carry it out. Entrepreneurship is about innovations being implemented.

How Real Businesspeople Identify Entrepreneurship

"Altimese Nichole, the founder of NicholeNicole, shares: "Most are excited about becoming an entrepreneur, but when reality hits, they get discouraged. Entrepreneurship requires remaining dedicated beyond your feelings of enthusiasm to your objectives. Stay on the course and bear in mind your 'why.'

The entrepreneurship concept of Christopher Molaro

"Christopher Molaro, Founder and CEO of NeuroFlow, says, "Entrepreneurship means being the one who is willing to take a risk, working hard enough to sacrifice everything else around you, all in the name of solving issues when no one else is able or has the motivation.

Entrepreneur Jolijt Tamanaha, meaning

For the Director of Marketing and Finance for Fresh Prints, Jolijt Tamanaha, who shares: 'Entrepreneurs find their way down an endless list of grit, ambition, and energy issues, the sense of entrepreneurship is a bit different? Being an entrepreneur, though intense, means you get to live life learning an amazing amount and optimize your effect on the world because you get to tackle the most challenging problems.

Nicole Religious Faith

Here's how it is broken down by Nicole Faith, Founder of 10 Carat Creations: "Being an entrepreneur means having a plan and vision but still succeeding or trying to succeed when the plan falls apart, and only your vision is left." It also means knowing when to give up, especially if your idea doesn't work because of outside forces.

James Sandoval James Sandoval

According to James Sandoval, Measure Match Founder and CEO: "Being an entrepreneur means diving headlong into your own [probably very risky] venture, working hard, long hours, often alone, to find a path to success and never, ever giving up."

Mike Kim Kim

Mike Kim, KPOP Foods' co-founder, and COO reveal what entrepreneurship really is about. "For the faint-hearted, entrepreneurship is not. I'm a member of the US Army. I was in battle, and I encountered a lot of tough conditions. Nevertheless, I can honestly tell starting a business has been just as complicated, albeit in different ways.

Although no one's life may be in immediate danger, with no rest, the battles you face on your entrepreneurial journey may last for years. It takes tremendous amounts of action, perseverance, and conviction to build a successful company. You'll find the experience rich in rewards if you understand this and want to continue.

Chapter 1: Understanding entrepreneurship

Entrepreneurial capitalism is important for entrepreneurship to thrive. Entrepreneurial capitalism is characterized as private capital, investing in private startups with the potential to generate a viable harvest. For thousands of years, the notion of entrepreneurship has been overused and, in some cases, underused in our modern culture and in the history of economic science. What are entrepreneurs doing, then? What makes an entrepreneur effective? In supporting entrepreneurial capitalism, what is the role of governments? The majority would accept that the answers are not easy.

An entrepreneur is one who organizes a new venture, manages it, and assumes the associated risk, beginning from virtually nothing. Theoretically, entrepreneurship encompasses many subdisciplines, including small business or lifestyle entrepreneurs, potential entrepreneurs with high growth, experienced or serial entrepreneurs, corporate entrepreneurs, and social entrepreneurs. The main goals of an entrepreneur are profit and development, and to achieve them, they will employ structured strategic management practices.

Entrepreneurship starts with the study of an idea and potential. In the thrilling process of bringing together a small team of innovative people in search of a limited chance before someone else does, the significance can be found. However, becoming an entrepreneur means taking on risks as well. "No such an entrepreneur-led "venture team" can handle all the "important capital resources" needed, equipment, raw materials, and startup funds, because it needs a bridging of the resource gap to pursue such an opportunity. Prudent decision-making allows the entrepreneur to behave in a way that is compatible with the reduction and creation of risk.

The thrilling appeal of entrepreneurship attracts a lot of people to aspire to be entrepreneurs who are just not ready for it. This is, actually, one explanation why so many new startups fail, because not all startups are successful, obviously. For the millions of US sole proprietorships, the total annual net revenue for the first year is less than $50,000. And during a typical year, about 25 percent of these projects do not make a penny of profit.

Faced with these odds, since they are willing to take major risks, entrepreneurs show many of the characteristics of the early pioneers. In places where the majority say it can not be achieved, they invent. For lengthy periods of time, they work extremely long hours and even experience personal issues, all for the thrill of creating a product or constructing an enterprise. Their passion brings to their ventures a concentrated emphasis. Most of them have the capacity to sell themselves and their ideas, but few know that they can't do it all on their own.

Basically, entrepreneurs begin with nothing more than an idea and a blueprint or roadmap. They build "venture teams" in this "entrepreneurial life cycle" that have the capacity and capital to grow ideas to the point at which the startup can sustain itself and produce a healthy cash flow internally. They usually start from scratch; they have no offices, no distributors, no machines, no manufacturers, and no customers. Their job at hand is to rapidly achieve a "critical mass" by bringing together all the ideas and money and still making a profit as fast as possible somehow. In this entrepreneurial life cycle, experienced or "serial" entrepreneurs are masters. They understand how to overcome challenges, and they know how to rebound from roadblocks and setbacks.

Everyone who sees a new one is an entrepreneur company concept and creates an enterprise to harvest the opportunity; the company life cycle is called the activity involved in that search. A sequence of fits, starts and brainstorms are very much the entrepreneurial life cycle. The ability to maneuver through uncharted waters and, when faced with a difficult challenge, carry on is what makes an entrepreneur successful. "The economist Joseph Schumpeter said, "The entrepreneur gets stuff done as the inventor creates ideas.

It is a challenging job to educate aspiring entrepreneurs, one that is complicated because of the lack of any consistent career trends. There is also really no such thing as a "true entrepreneurial profile" to benefit from. Entrepreneurs come from a range of academic backgrounds. It does not necessarily take an MBA graduate to successfully start and harvest a company. Entrepreneurs have a peculiar way of thought, reasoning, and obsessing over the ability to reap. They build teams that are leadership-balanced in a holistic approach, injecting creativity, inspiration, dedication, enthusiasm, collaboration, and vision.

Some claim that entrepreneurship on an icy road is like driving fast. It needs unique market knowledge through domain experience, anticipation, and "traction" with sales to survive the journey. More significantly, It's a matter of finding the right balance between the opportunity and the individual.

Entrepreneurs are rewarded with the freedom to do as they want, the ability to monitor and reduce risks selectively; they are rewarded with the ability to produce limitless amounts of revenue. It takes a strong, solid plan and a far-reaching vision to achieve this.

Why does entrepreneurship matter so much?

Entrepreneurs build jobs: Jobs will not exist without entrepreneurs. Entrepreneurs are taking the risk of recruiting themselves. Their determination to continue the growth of their company inevitably leads to new jobs being generated. Many more jobs are produced as their company continues to expand.

Entrepreneurs innovate: some of today's society's best inventions have emerged from corporations. The advances in technology derive from the need to solve a problem, build efficiencies, or change the environment. There is typically an entrepreneur to thank for it in times when there is a further development in technology.

Businesspeople drive change: Businesspeople dream big. So, inevitably, some of their theories are going to change worldwide. They could develop a new product that addresses a burning issue or take on the task of discovering something that has never been explored before. Through their goods, concepts, or organizations, many seek to make the world better.

Entrepreneurs offer society: while some have this idea of the wealthy being bad and selfish, they also do more than the average citizen for the common good. They earn more cash and also pay more in taxes, which helps to finance social programs. Entrepreneurs for various causes are some of the leading donors to charities and nonprofits. Some are trying to invest their money in the creation of strategies to help disadvantaged people have access to things that we take for granted, such as clean drinking water and decent health care.

Entrepreneurs contribute to national income: Entrepreneurship in an economy creates new capital. The development of new markets and new wealth is allowed by new ideas and improved goods or services from entrepreneurs.

Reasons why individuals are becoming entrepreneurs:

To change the world: Many entrepreneurs are working to improve the world. They eventually create a brand in the service of others, whether entrepreneurs believe in space exploration, reducing poverty, or producing a realistic yet game-changing product. Some entrepreneurs use their company as a means of rapidly raising capital to funnel into their noble causes.

They don't want a manager: businessmen also fail to have a boss. Maybe they feel suffocated and held back. Some entrepreneurs may find that they have a way of doing things more efficiently. The lack of artistic freedom could be hated by others. Ultimately, to succeed on their own terms, they become drawn to entrepreneurship. Check out ten visible signs for yourself that you should be working.

They want flexible hours: For those who need flexible hours, entrepreneurship is common. Many people with disabilities, for instance, also love entrepreneurship, as it encourages them to work while they can. Without feeling bad about it, parents may raise their children at home or pick them up from school. Students have the freedom to work around their challenging timetables and tonnes of courses.

They want to work from anywhere: entrepreneurship is common among those who do not want to be bound to a particular location, along with flexibility in working hours. Every day, entrepreneurs may not want to work from the same place, as this can get boring quickly.

They can't get a job: When they can't get a job, many find a way into entrepreneurship. They create fresh opportunities for themselves instead of being defeated by their situation. The summer after graduation, a new graduate could start an online store to build up their resume. In the coronavirus economy, a parent who has been laid off might start a business to ensure that they can continue to feed their family while maintaining a roof over their heads.

They don't fit into the business climate: entrepreneurs sometimes complain their growth is limited by stuffy corporate environments. In a corporate environment, you will spot an entrepreneur as they typically strive to gain more control over their position and better understand how everything works together.

They're curious: Entrepreneurs want to find the answer to the question,' what if...' They're experimental and love learning. To advance their expertise, they frequently read business books. So, of course, they are drawn to entrepreneurship because doing it helps them to learn the most in the shortest period of time. Their curiosity enables their continued growth.

They're ambitious: entrepreneurs are made to be those who enjoy achieving challenging targets and milestones. As there is no limit to what they can do, entrepreneurs are continually finding their ventures growing larger and greater than they have ever expected. They find the workaround to their target as challenges come up. They are comparable.

Ideas for Entrepreneurs

As a startup entrepreneur, depending on the business experience you already have, and what you are able to learn, there are so many ideas you can try. To get you started, here are a handful of business ideas:
- Owner of the Ecommerce Shop
- A freelancer (write a blog, accountant, designer)
- TEACHING (online courses, author)
- The maker of App (chatbots, social media apps)
- The company focused on service (food delivery, cleaning, dog walking)
- Consultant-based firm (wedding planner, life coach)
- Renting apartments (Airbnb)
- Businesses in Marketing (influencer marketing, SEO brands, PR firms)
- Marketing with associates (Amazon Affiliate, Clickbank, etc.)
- Blogger (Product reviews, niche blog, magazine)
- Vlogger (start a YouTube channel, Twitch)
- Flipper (domain name, website, house)
- +Translator
- Economy Gig (driver, Fiverr)
- Real Estate Officer (condos, houses, commercial)
- Photographer Photograph (product photography, sell photos)
- Broker of Stocks (buying and selling stocks)
- Tutor for
- Flipper for website
- Company of resellers

Entrepreneurship

1.1 Top Qualities of a Successful Entrepreneur

Company is an art, and not all people know how to master it. In order to be a good entrepreneur, some individuals have inborn qualities, while others strive to improve these qualities.

All will benefit from continuing to work on these essential attributes, no matter which of these definitions suits you best.

Here are a good entrepreneur's top five qualities:

1. Resolute support and enthusiasm

Passion is the first and foremost characteristic of a good entrepreneur.

If they do not have a passion for achieving the goal, no one can accomplish anything. As a result of this utter ambition, as he takes on new challenges and learns new things in order to accomplish that aim, inspiration begins to build in the mind of an entrepreneur.

When he or she progresses towards the target, inspiration keeps blood flowing, helping an entrepreneur to retain optimism and conquer obstacles. This is why, in a whole new way, a good entrepreneur is passionate and inspired.

2. Discipline of oneself

This is one of a good entrepreneur's most important features.

If an entrepreneur can perform important tasks (whether or not he feels up to it), then he will be able to achieve greater success.

Self-discipline simply means mastering the inner self and inner feelings to build a sense of duty, which encourages self-direction, to get the job done.

3. Capability for risk-taking

All about taking chances is about entrepreneurship. To achieve greater success, entrepreneurs have the potential to take greater risks, but not all risk-takers are good entrepreneurs.

A good entrepreneur knows when to take risks and which risks to the business or himself would be advantageous or detrimental.

Before taking risks, all entrepreneurs prepare and make a plan B (in case of any loss or mishap) and set down an acceptable basis for the consequences of the risks.

4. Creative thought for creative thinking

A good entrepreneur is an innovative thinker continuously streaming through her mind with loads of ideas. This dramatic ability to think of a wide variety of new ideas allows an entrepreneur in a special, innovative way to start various types of business.

5. Persevere

Persistence is an effective entrepreneur's most fundamental and necessary attribute since even good entrepreneurs suffer setbacks and hurdles. Yet you're able to pick yourself up and keep going towards your goals with persistence.

These five attributes will assist you in becoming a successful entrepreneur you are aspiring to be. Look for these qualities in yourself, and for the good of yourself and your company, continue to improve every day.

A strong entrepreneur's most important attributes
In this article, we will tell you about an entrepreneur's top 10 main qualities that make them successful.

Discipline

If you don't have self-discipline, so succeeding as an entrepreneur is very difficult for you. Discipline and patience for managing the operation is one thing that all well-known businessmen possess. Performance for entrepreneurs of this quality is assured.

Risk-Taking Action

An entrepreneur is a willing person to sacrifice anything in order to make a business profit. Without any guarantee of profits, all businessmen invest their efforts and resources. Risk-taking is one of the key characteristics that should be preserved in order to climb to the top.

Minded-Open-Minded

Do you know that an entrepreneur sees each situation as a business opportunity? That's why they constantly generate ideas about workflows & performance. Simply put, their open-mindedness helps them to come close to their targets.

Creativeness

Another valuable quality that an entrepreneur possesses is to use his/her imagination to build ties between difficult situations. It allows them to find ways that help them easily overcome difficult situations.

Ethnic Job

You're not even going to find a single wealthy businessman who doesn't have good work ethics. Most of them come to the office early and work until the late hours. In addition, they are able to give up their holidays to fulfill their duties.

Feel Path

The next attribute of an entrepreneur is getting a good understanding of the direction they are moving in. The reasoning behind that is the time they spend on training and preparing for future plans.

Skills for Solid People

There is a solid range of communication skills that marketers have to sell goods that give their workers inspiration. They know the method for empowering their workers to develop the business.

Love

Passion for the company is the next significant characteristic of an entrepreneur. In those people, you can see an immense amount of love for their work. It helps them to excel in business at a higher level.

Action Oriented-Oriented

Their action-oriented nature is another attribute that entrepreneurs keep in mind. You can see that all of them easily think and make choices. There is a total probability that you can see a great form of decision-making discipline in those individuals.

Competitive

In order to become competitive in the industry, entrepreneurs remain prepared to deal with the competitions they have to face. In reality, after understanding the rivals, you'll see them entering the enterprise. They know how to win, with good intent, from others.

Things that businessmen should know before starting a business

In this post, prior to starting a business in detail, we will tell you about the top 7 things to know. Let's check it out below in detail:

Investment isn't all.

In the early days of Entrepreneurship, no denying money is an important thing, but it is not appropriate to achieve success. A strong business plan that can create consistent cash flow is needed. In addition, it is ideal to have adequate resources to successfully implement the plan.

Target clients & their needs

Without clients, no company can succeed. That's why targeting them and identifying their requirements is vital. Train the staff in such a way as they can remain involved with their needs in order to do so.

Go for the business of the right.

Do you know that selecting the perfect company is the greatest difference between success and business? No matter what you try, if you select a business that isn't right for you, the chances of earning a profit are very low.

Never in the Past Stuck

Always follow the current methods for achieving company success. If you continue to use things from the past, then we suggest you get ready for failure. With 1990's marketing campaigns in 2019, for example, you can't succeed. To achieve new heights, it is important to remain updated.

Don't hire People Known.

It is one thing to have a friend as a business partner, but hiring them as an employee is a different thing. People believe the two are the same thing, but that's not the truth. You're going to find it tough to deal with them like a boss. It can lead to the creation of uncomfortable situations that need to be avoided. So, please do not hire friends or business relatives at all.

Don't fear failure,

According to great entrepreneurs, the fear of failure is the biggest issue that keeps businessmen away from success. It's not easy to take the path of entrepreneurship, as you may fail many times. Never take failure as stress and keep working towards your vision.

Find a Real Mentor

It won't be less than a blessing to have an entrepreneurship mentor. Everyone wants to have someone who can guide them on a successful journey. It does not say, however, that you should follow anyone blindly. Always select very carefully and wisely for your mentor. Go for the individual in your respective company that has a great track record. It can turn out to be a disaster that should be avoided by following YouTube mentors who only know how to talk.

Any of entrepreneurship's big benefits

Chance of job development

Entrepreneurship

Moving on the road of entrepreneurship provides a sign of courage for people to be able to accomplish their goals and see progress in their careers. No one may interfere with the process of making decisions that allow the person to be their boss.

It simply means he/she has to come and take risks out of their comfort zone. The rise in demand may lead to the process of making money.

Few Restrictions

There is pure freedom given to the person by entrepreneurship as they focus on themselves rather than on others. It can't, by any means, be contrasted with any career opportunity. In possession of a human, the complete power of destiny remains.

Compared to working for others, the thing we want to tell the individual has to deal with very fewer limits in entrepreneurship.

Endless Chances

The person can discover tonnes of possibilities that work can never bring as an entrepreneur. Apart from the opportunity to earn cash, you can explore the places you really want. A person has the gears for all things ranging from expanding the company and even re-training the staff or yourself.

The person can be the maker of destiny, allowing them to explore a variety of horizons.

Climate Excited

Entrepreneurship creates a brand new type of world with lots of enthusiasm. No doubt, as compared to a professional job, the worker has to work harder and longer. In the early days of entrepreneurship, there is a lot of work involved.

However, it would be worthwhile to fuel your enthusiasm to feel the amount of excitement you will experience during long working days.

Perks for vacation

This is, without a doubt, the greatest value that can be enjoyed when practicing entrepreneurship. The time and date of the vacation may be chosen by a self-employed person without any need for approval.

In addition, they would have the freedom to function according to the hours that best fit their needs. As per their schedule, they are free to choose working timings.

Improved communication with the Community

As we have already said, entrepreneurship provides more versatility, which allows individuals more time to get active in the Community. When it comes to the variety of ways one can support society, the list is very open.

These kinds of possibilities allow them to build a network that can be very helpful to the company. In addition, it helps to improve the character as well as to further market the brand. With this versatility, individuals may develop a long-term partnership with community members, clients, and colleagues.

Any of entrepreneurship's big disadvantages

No Income Guaranteed

Compared to working for others, the greatest downside of entrepreneurship has a guaranteed paycheck. One may assume that there are chances of being fired from the job, but on a daily basis, the income is credited.

It demonstrates that entrepreneurship works both for the entrepreneur and his/her families with low financial stability. On top of that, the family of employers has a wide range of benefits.

Long Shifts Working

For most of the time, set working hours are another benefit that daily work is provided to a person. In addition, overpay is given in most jobs if a worker works for long hours.

This independence, though, doesn't come while working as an entrepreneur. Without earning too much money, one can operate for long shifts of even 16 to 20 hours. It can be considered one of the major disadvantages of entrepreneurship.

Degree of High Patience

False statements on the internet are one of the most business-related issues. Many individuals report loads of income by doing much less work. There is no lack of networking individuals who claim to receive far more than a million a year. The truth, however, is very difficult because you have to wait for years to earn US$ 10,000 in the first year of your company.

The thing we want to say is that entrepreneurship takes a lot of patience from people that not everybody has.

Solid amounts of stress

People complain about getting a hard job and say it's an easy task to do for business. The truth is radically different because there is a very fresh and solid form of stress involved in entrepreneurship. In the early years of this company, there are lots of failures involved, so the entrepreneur should be ready for it.

Moreover, if the income from the company is not reliable, stress will reach a whole new stage.

Implications of Tax

No matter what country an entrepreneur is in, the company is involved in a certain collection of tax-related conditions. This implies that the person must obey the tax rules laid down by the jurisdiction. In the beginning, most people have pretty little knowledge of taxation, particularly young people.

It is therefore important that the individual also understands the set of tax rules that are laid down in their country. A very important thing to have is to have a comprehensive knowledge of them.

1.2 The role of creativity in entrepreneurship

One of the things that every leader and entrepreneur needs are imagination.

In reality, in problem-solving systems, individuals seldom applaud entrepreneurs for their innovation. Creativity is also seen as the stronghold of those in the world of writing and design.

Creativity's position in entrepreneurship

Creativity reduces the limits of an investor's mentality and ability set.

A lot of people, however, equate imagination with a lack of discipline and feel that chaos can be induced. Leadership, in comparison, is more about power and order.

As such, innovation and entrepreneurship form a perfect mix. To run a profitable business no longer requires number-crunching abilities and practicality.

Creativity has been an important component of good company acumen over time. Lack of imagination could easily pull your company into the stagnation process.

Here's why innovation is important to entrepreneurs.

Overall high success

There is a myth that to do what they need in life, and people only need knowledge.

For young entrepreneurs, though, it takes time to understand that innovation still plays an integral role.

Sadly, many learning institutions emphasize knowledge rather than creative thinking. Perhaps it may be that analytical intelligence is measurable, while imagination can be difficult to detect. Nevertheless, dynamics are shifting, and the value of having innovative people on board is starting to be understood by entrepreneurs. If you appropriately harness and shape their talents, innovative employees can be a game-changer in your company.

Step up efficiency

In order to distinguish new and useful ideas, imagination helps an entrepreneur to disconnect from the consumer and venture into uncharted territories.

Therefore, it has become important to cultivate creative skills for both leaders and workers.

In order to help their employees explore new strategies and ideas, entrepreneurs have the requisite technical tools, such as visual communication, which is frequently mistaken for video conferencing.

This is potentially an incredibly cost-effective technique to improve efficiency in the workplace. Innovation and imagination lead an entrepreneur to the road to success.

Exploit the opportunity for workers

You're probably using just half of the ability of your employee by not promoting innovation in the workplace.

Fortunately, the ocean of new ideas that remain untapped and latent is gradually being realized by entrepreneurs.

Improved financial strategies, improved profitability, and rapid decision-making will benefit from tapping all these opportunities. Creativity also helps a company to remain ahead of the curve.

Boundaries Overcome

Creativity helps entrepreneurs to discover these path-breaking discoveries.

As such, it is important to allow collisions to take place and blur to transcend boundaries set by disciplines.

It is easier for an entrepreneur to get new ideas on solving a financial or organizational problem in this way.

Creativity helps an entrepreneur to connect various aspects and to extrapolate realistic alternatives from unrelated ideas.

Foster critical thought

Creativity is increasingly turning out to be one of the best ways to alleviate issues plaguing companies today.

When combined with highly disciplined and concentrated thinking, problem-solving works best. In either a divergent or convergent thought mode, entrepreneurs may think.

In-depth research requires convergent thinking and helps an entrepreneur to find the most viable solution to a managerial or financial challenge.

This encourages entrepreneurs to use different sources of knowledge, such as accounting software and computer systems.

Divergent thinking, on the other hand, promotes innovation by encouraging business owners to consider potential solutions to the same problem.

While both thought styles can be merged by entrepreneurs, divergent thinking ensures that an organization gets the best resolution.

Foster imagination

Manufacturers build exclusive products to not only meet but also exceed consumer needs.

As such, to ensure their goods are important and useful to consumers, entrepreneurs need to be careful.

Although it will be difficult to spot this from the outset, as the concept becomes a reality, things start to become more apparent.

This is essentially the moment that an entrepreneur starts to grasp how creativity and invention vary. The definition refers to a new, unique idea, while innovation is an idea that is as distinctive and useful as the original.

To be innovative, you need to be imaginative and interpret an idea differently. That way, translating an idea into a fact is easier.

Entrepreneurship Creativity: Value and Forms

Creativity refers to the fundamental source of inventiveness and can lead to the development of new companies and to improve the company's existing products to become more efficient and competitive in the marketplace. A mixture of innovation and technology in entrepreneurship practices to commercialize the concept of goods and services is helpful in improving entrepreneurship.

Importance of entrepreneurial creativity

Do you know what variables have made creativity so important to the entrepreneurial process and work perfectly in an entrepreneur's working life? For some reasons, as given below, this leads to success:

Innovative ideas were created: the whole entrepreneurship process revolved around the development and discovery of some innovative ideas. When an entrepreneur becomes innovative, effective, and in favor of the company, they can stay ahead of the curve and beat the competition in a very appropriate way. It is a kind of learning ability that some people possess to explore some inventive ideas and thoughts that can make a huge difference and help the company to remain on the hit list at all times.

Novel ways to design and enhance products: Innovation is all about making improvements to products or services in such a way that something new is produced. There are high chances of improvement in any product, but to know0 what is missing in the products, you just need some kind of creative thinking. Only by a visionary entrepreneur can this thing be tested.

Thinking out of the world: Innovation is called the purpose and imagination of creating something new with creative ideas. Imagination is often important to cross the boundaries between normal and special and to come up with something that can help you think beyond the box. The imaginative visionary still thinks outside of the world and substitutes innovative solutions for conventional solutions. In order to get some opportunity, imagination meant to be produces something new, fascinating, and flexible.

Searching for the same trends, but the areas are different: somehow, we still go for the same procedures all the time due to monotonous routine and surroundings. The relation between various and unrelated subjects enables imagination to take place and to generate some good entrepreneurial ideas. The development of new niches comes from the combination of numerous ideas and fields that can provide a creative and fascinating intersection. There is no fear of putting the different disciplines together, but some may have interesting ideas through the combining of the various fields.

Development of new innovative and entrepreneurial niches: Exploring the new facets of traditional business in entrepreneurship is crucial. It can be achieved in different ways, such as adjusting production processes, distribution methods, or making certain improvements to the service or product. In market strategies, all these shifts make a huge difference and give rise to a new niche.

Startup success is not enough: often, entrepreneurs get some initial ideas that build in people's minds a creative picture of the entrepreneur and assume that in the future, it is not important to be creative again. But this is not at all necessary in order to thrive in the avenue of business as innovation keeps a company ahead of the curve.

Things keep changing all the time, and you need to find something creative all the time to stabilize the uniqueness of your organization when you find a new idea instead of the old one. Going forward with some thoughts and suggestions is an important part of every organization and has paved the way for success.

A table full of untraditional ideas: if someone does a specific job in the same way, conventional thought leads to the same practice for a long time. But if you want to win, you've got to have to question traditional approaches and bring something new to the market. Disruption is a breed of imagination.

Apple Inc, for instance, is transforming people's vision of how they look forward to the cell phone and what the company has found. Nobody ever believed they could be mobile phones something new and have changed a device's entire mental picture.

Apple is changing the whole definition, and then someone learned about "phone," and then a shadow like a computer appeared. That is called the creativity that fills the table and, by nature, reveals an entrepreneur's creativity.

Stand out from the crowd: something extraordinary is a startup with massive success that can set an example that you are totally special from others. He wanted to get out of the crowd.

For example, when individuals think about the reasons behind an application crash on a mobile device, the entrepreneur should find the perfect way to deal with the issue. For individuals to deal with all these problems was rather boring and annoying, and the answer seems absolutely incredible. Afterward, individuals use ideas and often provide input. If the device is perfectly fine, then it creates the entrepreneur's status quo and offers a breath of relief.

Pushing the potential and never settling down: If the company runs smoothly and the entrepreneur is happy with the whole operation, then it is also very risky and monotonous. Even if the company is doing well, it doesn't mean you can't do better.

It switches the advantage in the competitor's hand, however, and they can innovate anything to bring down your company and appear traditional. Never settle, as it is not your place of work, but the business. In the meantime, the organization still wants some innovation, your goods, your understanding, and ideas.

Become a solution: not only is innovation a flash of inspiration, but also great designers, artists, and authors struggle in the face of creativity. The only way to make it right is continuously working on the problem.

In certain situations, it can take a few tries, and others can take days and even months, too. But there is no reason to settle down, no matter how much time it takes when you can do better. An ideal logo, for instance, takes 15 to 20 days to get finished with all the precise color combinations.

The importance of innovation in an entrepreneur's life is important to consider, as it is essential for all facets of the organization and plays an outstanding role. Have you ever experienced the psychology behind creativity? It is not easy to comprehend as it is of various kinds. When others believe it's a kind of innate ability or ability that very few people have, and some think you should learn how to become more inventive. But it doesn't really like that, either.

1.3 How to Become an Entrepreneur

What is a businessman?

An entrepreneur is a concept in this country that we hear a lot, but do we really know what it is? We think of company owners of all sorts when we think of entrepreneurs. Restaurants, owners of car shops, digital startups, self-employed photographers, all of which will qualify as occupations for entrepreneurs.

What is the determining element, however?

The phrase businessman comes from the French word for entrepreneur 'to undertake.' No, not an undertaker who digs, but a person who, with the ultimate aim of financial benefit, undertakes risk and initiative.

Entrepreneurs are described as someone who, with the aim of financial benefit, takes a risk.

Clearly, making money is not the only motivator for entrepreneurs, but the underlying trend for all entrepreneurs is risk-taking, typically in the form of financial investment.

In order to create something that will last, entrepreneurs are still working. One of the distinguishing factors for an entrepreneur is taking the required steps to build a company that, when properly run, can continue to make money for them when they are not operating. For example, a cafe owner can make money when the cafe does business, even though she's picking up children from school.

Freelancers vs. Businesspeople

Millions of people have adopted their skills online and become freelancers in today's digitally linked world. When they come to work on their own terms, they take jobs, usually in writing, design, or as a consultant of some kind. But are entrepreneurs freelancers?

Freelancers have many of the same characteristics (more on that below) as entrepreneurs, but they don't create anything that will actually make a profit when they sleep, take a holiday, or leave for the day. Although the two words are relatively ambiguous, they are different. A freelancer isn't an entrepreneur by other standards.

How do you know if it is right for you to be an entrepreneur?

How can you say if an entrepreneur's life is for you? Some of the attributes, qualities, and values that most successful entrepreneurs share are certain. While they do not guarantee success, some entrepreneurial features lay a strong foundation of risk-taking and reward for life.

Entrepreneurs respect freedom first and foremost. They want to be bosses of their own, set a schedule of their own, and run their own lives. While businessmen have hundreds, thousands, or millions of people, they are people who hate the thought of a boss controlling their job; they are called "customers."

Entrepreneurs are based on themselves. They enjoy being accountable for their own results and are proud of creating something greater than themselves.

They must also be in a position to manage risk. If the prospect of not being paid on a regular basis, struggling to sell your product, or simply falling flat on your face scares you to paralysis, you could have trouble coping with the up-and-down nature of entrepreneurship.

Long-lasting entrepreneurs are also frugal because of the higher levels of risk. Despite popular culture telling us that champagne is popping up and cruising on luxurious yachts, most company owners are savers, not spenders. This was illustrated by Dr. Thomas Stanley's study and published in The Millionaire Next Door (1996), which found that the majority of millionaires in this nation are small business owners (not lawyers, physicians, or bankers) and are daily savers. 81% buy their cars instead of leasing them, and 90% spend less than $45,000 on purchasing them. The book may need updating, but as an entrepreneur, it highlights the ever-important need for frugal living.

How to Become a Contractor

So, what would you do to become a businessman? In order to become an entrepreneur, what are the steps? There are many different directions you can take because of the many forms of entrepreneurs. The owner of a delivery agency, for instance, does not follow the exact same direction as an interior decorator. But there are several similar actions that should be taken by all of them.

These are, in general, the steps that you would take to become an entrepreneur:
Phase 1: Find your Niche or Industry
Phase 2: The Market Research
Stage Three: Educate Yourself
Phase 4: Slowly develop your company

Phase 1: Find your Niche or Industry

It's the most obvious first step to discovering your unique niche. Many individuals want to become entrepreneurs, but they do not know what organization they should be interested in.

Your specialty would be something you have been working on for years, more often than not. Home remodeling and renovation can be your area if you have been a carpenter for a local construction company. You already have a good awareness of how to run a food service company if you have worked at a restaurant for several years. A perfect place to start searching for your niche is your current experience.

It will also help if your niche is enjoyed by you. You have to enjoy what you do in order to have years of success. Ultimately, cash will not be a big enough motivator to keep you going sixty to seventy hours a week to help the company. To keep you motivated, you'll need more than money; you'll need a reason.

Phase 2: The Market Research

You can also study the market open, evaluating the region for demand and need.

You would like to open a fine Your hometown's Italian restaurant. Are the other restaurants successful? In your town, is there another great restaurant? Can local customers afford to eat in a high-end restaurant, or do they prefer a more humble place to eat? Do they still like Italy's food?

Seeking the answers and more to these questions will be key to your long-term success.

Stage 3: Educate Yourself

In popular culture, there's a common misconception that wealthy, self-made entrepreneurs never graduate from college. However, the numbers don't back this up. Over 95 percent of entrepreneurs in high-growth industries have at least a bachelor's degree, according to a team of researchers from Duke, Akron, and Southern California.

Phase 4: Slowly develop your company

Many aspiring entrepreneurs think that the sign of a good company is quick, rapid growth. Most firms, however, are constructed slowly, over years and even decades. Entrepreneurs would build slowly wherever possible, beginning with the very first sale and crawling forward. Slow construction helps you to learn and make improvements before plunging headfirst into the business. Dealing with new circumstances offers valuable on-the-job experience in entrepreneurship that you can not receive from any formal degree. In certain ways, managers would retain their day jobs while constructing the company in their spare time.

Earnings opportunity for entrepreneurs

In estimating earnings for entrepreneurs, there is complexity. Nevertheless, Business News Daily revealed the average entrepreneurial salary to be $68,000, down from $72,00 the year before, citing a 2013 study by American Express Available. The study also found that a second job is employed by 15 percent of entrepreneurs, indicating that these entrepreneurs fail to achieve profitability.

The ultimate challenge for a statistician would be to try to calculate the entrepreneurship wage. There are so many factors, including savings, taxation, certifications, the buying of goods, and payroll, and all of these can drain an entrepreneur's earnings easily. So, while you can sell a product worth $2 million, that doesn't mean you're going to receive $2 million.

The large variations in the industry are another issue in forecasting entrepreneurial wages. Elon Musk, the founder of PayPal, Tesla Motors, and SpaceX, for instance, is an entrepreneur. The owners are also entrepreneurs of a local mom and pop diner. Today, maybe Mom and Pop have savings of a few million and are very happy, but the odds are high that over the past 15 years, Musk has made much more money than Mom and Pop.

Becoming a good entrepreneur tips

To improve your chances of success as an entrepreneur, there are many things that you can do.

To maintain a company, entrepreneurs need many instruments, skills, and characteristics, and one of the most important things they can do is to maintain positivity. No, this doesn't mean the path to a good company is happy-thinking; it means having a positive outlook, even though times are down. A negative-minded person would focus on their mistakes when something goes wrong and perhaps call it quits, while a positive mind would look at the loss and decide what went wrong and how to fix it.

A successful entrepreneur, both from a personal and professional viewpoint, will also be focused on learning and developing. This means receiving, if necessary, the latest certifications, taking classes to develop communication skills, or subscribing to business newsletters that provide valuable knowledge for future choices. A common theme for successful entrepreneurs is consciously and deliberately striving towards change and evolving their efforts.

Entrepreneurs would also hold separate personal and job finances. It is recommended that entrepreneurs have different bank accounts for money that belongs to the company and money that belongs to the individual in order to set budgets and pay themselves properly. This may sound like a small difference, but it can influence how and how you spend your work.

Another significant technique is to establish a support network, both emotional and business-related. Entrepreneurs have a lot to think about, and it will help you concentrate on running your company by getting some of these tasks off your hands. A support network that includes an accounting or financial specialist, a marketing consultant of some kind and a mentor that can offer advice and guidance would be available to many entrepreneurs.

Pitfalls to avoid

Entrepreneurs need to avoid several pitfalls, and while some of them are obvious, some of them can creep up and ruin your future. Before even making your first sale, these traps can come, or they can come after you have finally begun to construct your success.

Efficient entrepreneurs would tell you, literally across the board, to stop debt wherever possible. Some will tell you, like Mark Cuban, to escape debt altogether. According to Cubans, you are already doomed to fail if you start a business by borrowing money. A more moderate view on the debt would be taken by other entrepreneurs, saying instead that debt should be held to a minimum. It is difficult to become an entrepreneur with no income, but high levels of debt are a pitfall for entrepreneurs.

It may sound counterintuitive, but when it's not properly handled, rapid growth can actually be a pitfall for entrepreneurs. When an organization is too busy, they can not be able to process all the orders, weaknesses in management may begin to expose themselves, and communication may begin to break down. Outcome? Until the bottom falls out, a gradual decline in sales. It is important to be prepared for success with flexible management models and quality control.

Over-dependency on a single source of income is another pitfall to avoid. By not having a single client represent more than 25 percent of their profits, a successful entrepreneur can prevent over-dependence. What happens when they decide to avoid doing business if a single customer or client constitutes too much of the sales? A large amount of your revenue is lost to you.

During the financial crisis of 2008, this idea was seen on a wide scale. American Axle produced components mainly for General Motors, with GM accounting for approximately 76 percent of their sales. American Axle was almost forced into bankruptcy after the automaker drastically cut orders. It will help you prevent this pitfall by getting a diverse client base.

There are other risks to avoid, including internal strife and high turn-around of staff, but a good entrepreneur will keep going forward with good management, a sound business strategy, and quality support.

Becoming an entrepreneur: is it that risky, really?

This involves long days, working weekends, and dealing with a number of unknowns that make most individuals leave before they begin.

Risk is always the main reason people avoid becoming an entrepreneur, but consider this: anyone who works for a corporation has one source of income: their employer; there are several different sources for an entrepreneur. If the employee is laid off, they are out of a paycheck, but they have a lot more to fall back on if an entrepreneur loses a client. Being an entrepreneur can potentially be one of the best professions possible when handled properly.

1.4 Types of Entrepreneurs: Understanding the Unique Differences

Entrepreneurs turn bold concepts into truth. They are generating jobs and contributing to the economy, but there are various types of entrepreneurs and, depending on their personality, skills, and atmosphere, each type tends to follow its own course.

Depending on the history, country, and even industry, the types of entrepreneurs differ, but the five most popular types are:
- The Innovators
- HUSTLERS
- Ministers
- Scientists
- Purchasers

Each of these various forms of entrepreneurs has its own business success rules, but in terms of financing, marketing, people, and even managing themselves, most entrepreneurs go through very similar struggles. Because of this, we have built the Community of Lonely Entrepreneurs to guide you with the coaching, experience, Community, encouragement, and resources you need to prosper. Start here for a free trial.

We break down all styles and theoretically clarify which category you can fall into if you have ever wondered what qualities an entrepreneur needs in order to be successful.

What's your sort of entrepreneur?

In our previous post, when we spoke about entrepreneurial characteristics, we highlighted how entrepreneurs need ambition, grit, and a great deal of self-confidence to succeed in business.

You will have to think differently to be a good entrepreneur and make the right choices, such as understanding when and how to find business advisors, marketing their goods online, educating the employees, and interacting effectively.

Knowing what sort of entrepreneur you are and are not will also offer insight into the things you are going to be good at, not good at, and how to bring your idea to life.

Entrepreneur Styles

Let's look at some different types of entrepreneurs, their positions, and how the company's performance is influenced by each type:

1. The Innovators

The kinds of entrepreneurs that are coming up with entirely new ideas and develop them into profitable companies are innovators.

These entrepreneurs, in most situations, change the way people think about and do things. These entrepreneurs tend to be highly passionate and obsessive, deriving their inspiration from their business idea's peculiar existence.

By choosing product differentiation tactics that make their business stand out from the crowd, creative entrepreneurs often find new ways to market their products. And it's not only standing out from the crowd sometimes but also forming a new crowd.

It would be an understatement to suggest that innovators like Steve Jobs, Google's Larry Page, and Microsoft founder Bill Gates were obsessed with their companies.

Advantages of becoming an entrepreneur with innovation:
- Get all the glory of the company's success (and take all the arrows)
- Establish the rules
- Face limited rivalry within the first days
- Disadvantages of becoming an entrepreneur with innovation:
- To bring a new idea to life, you will need a lot of capital to

Entrepreneurship

- Shareholders also face opposition from
- The success timeframe is longer,

The capacity of a creative entrepreneur to conceive a new way of thinking makes them stand out from the crowd and, in many instances, wildly successful, but it takes considerable money, persistence, and determination to bring true creativity to life.

2. The Entrepreneur from Hustler

Hustlers only work harder and are willing to get their hands dirty, unlike innovators, whose vision is the gas in their engine. Hustlers often start small and worry about dedication as opposed to raising capital to grow their businesses. With the aim of being bigger in the future, these types of entrepreneurs concentrate on starting tiny.

Hustlers are inspired by their visions and will work incredibly hard to fulfill them. They prefer to be very concentrated and will get rid of all kinds of distractions, preferring short-term comfort over risks.

A prime example of a hustler is Mark Cuban. He began selling trash bags, newspapers, and even postage stamps in a very young company, and this hustle later produced a gold mine that was purchased by internet giant Yahoo!

Benefits of Being A Hustler
- The best of them will work out.
- They seem to have strong skin and don't give up easily.
- See anger and rejection as just a step in the process.

Disadvantages of A Hustler being
- Typically resistant to burn-out
- Wear out members of their team who don't have the same work ethic,
- The importance of raising capital is often not seen in contrast to only working harder.

While many hustlers never give up, many of them are willing to do anything to succeed, which means they have a lot of hits and misses, unfortunately. It takes a great deal longer than most other forms of entrepreneurs to fulfill their dreams.

3. Mimicers

The types of entrepreneurs who clone and strengthen those business concepts are imitators. In order to gain the upper hand in the industry, they are constantly searching for ways to make a specific product better.

Imitators are part innovators and part hustlers who do not adhere to other people's terms and have a lot of faith in themselves.

Benefits of Imitators
- It is simpler and less stressful to refine a business concept,
- You can easily equate the results to the original concept.
- Can learn and prevent errors made by the originator

Imitators' Drawbacks
- Their concepts are often linked to the initial definition.
- It's still necessary to play catch-up.

It can be a great way to grow a company by taking an existing concept and developing and enhancing it. It probably does not have as much danger as the innovator, but it might not be as sexy.

4. Scientist

Researchers will take their time to collect all the relevant information about it, even after having an idea. Failure is not an option for them because they have analyzed the concept from all angles.

Usually, research entrepreneurs believe in starting a business that is highly likely to succeed because they have put in detailed work to understand all aspects.

As a result, since they need the base of deep understanding, these types of entrepreneurs typically take a lot of time to introduce products to make choices. Much more than instincts and intuition, these entrepreneurs depend on data and facts. There should be no room for a researcher to make errors.

Benefits of being an enterprising researcher
- Plan for as many possible contingencies

- Write detailed, well-thought-out financial and business plans
- Focus on information and data rather than intestinal feelings
- Unless they feel like they know the market, they will not start.
- Minimizing the likelihood of business failure
- Disadvantages of being an entrepreneurial researcher
- Usually, sluggish movements
- Doesn't like risk and in a new venture, that can hamper progress

Although these kinds of entrepreneurs spend a lot of time researching and digging into the information to ensure their company's success, they can fall into the habit of obsessing over the numbers and focusing less on the business's running.

5. Purchasers

Their wealth is one thing that distinguishes buyers. These types of entrepreneurs have the resources to purchase promising companies and specialize in them.

Buyer entrepreneurs can locate a company and determine its feasibility, continue to purchase it, and find the most appropriate individual to manage it and develop it.

The benefits of being a Buyer
- It is less risky to purchase an already proven venture.
- Don't have to think about creativity too much,

Can concentrate on constructing something that has already passed through the construction of a base

- Have a market for your products already
- Inconveniences of becoming a customer
- For good companies usually pays a high price

You face the risk of buying companies that have issues that you think you can turn around.

Entrepreneurship Administrative

All the management strategies and functions of entrepreneurial activities are included in this group. It provides a very efficient way to address both present and potential circumstances that favor the company with merits and competitive advantage.

Administrative Entrepreneurship examples are few that can deliver an idea, such as quality control, job restructuring, innovative strategies for doing stuff, and consensus management. All these activities of this form of entrepreneurship optimize an organization's productivity and nuke the company's accomplishments and retain them in the dynamic marketplace.

For example, the Bangladesh government considers old-age pension schemes to be administrative entrepreneurship.

Entrepreneurship Opportunistic

This proverb defines this form of entrepreneurship and is the best of its kind illustration of the characteristics of Opportunistic Entrepreneurship.' Hit the iron when it is heavy.' The changes in the market often bring new opportunities, but not every business owner is able to recognize the possibilities and use them in a timely way. Opportunistic entrepreneurship is defined first-hand as the discovery, exploitation, and+++++++ success of potential opportunities.

Examples: Arthur Fry and Lan Hancock, FedEx, etc.

Entrepreneurship Acquisitive

Acquisitive Entrepreneurship is defined as this form of entrepreneurship from the selection of demonstrable characteristics and skills that enables and enhances the effectiveness of the organization and other related competencies. It equips the competitive environment with something that is of new importance and theoretically achieves the capabilities. This allows the organization to succeed in this world of rivalry. The argument illustrated is that any mistakes never discourage them from learning and discovering new talents but often inspire them all the time to try out those new things.

Entrepreneurship Incubative

Entrepreneurship

This Entrepreneurship category includes the generation of new kinds of ideas and projects within the organization's premises. It handles it in a constructive manner and guarantees the business firm's material benefit.

Some tech firms, such as Microsoft and Nokia, often find and promote innovative technology across a wide variety of products and differentiate between all types of products on the market to demonstrate this.

Entrepreneurship Imitative

This entrepreneurship imitates or copies operational goods and services under an arrangement with a franchise. It is a model that aims to disperse modern technology across the globe so that it can be used by individuals. It includes the introduction of current technology from all over the world and, with a few changes that fit the local requirements, it takes on existing technologies.

There's an example: Walton BD. Without being the real maker of those products, many products such as refrigerators, motorbikes, and other electronic products have been made. China, where mobile technologies are adapted and updated in order to take this to a new stage, can be another example.

Entrepreneurship in Private

The term Private Entrepreneurship is used to initiate entrepreneurship within the private sector. In order to encourage non-governmental initiatives in taking the ventures of Entrepreneurship, the government of each nation provides ample support services through public as well as private concerns. In addition, it accelerates economic growth and ensures a layer-to-mutual equilibrium.

Examples of private enterprise are Tesla, Disney, numerous grocery chains, and hospitals.

Entrepreneurship of the Public

Public Entrepreneurship is referred to as the entrepreneurship that the different development agencies fall under the government. In venture proposals, both industrialized and underdeveloped nations take action to resolve the preliminary shortage of private entrepreneurs. These are distinct from private entrepreneurs as they seek to address public and environmental problems under the government. They are, therefore, not social entrepreneurs since they are bound by the laws and regulations of the government.

Examples of public entrepreneurs are Hyman Rickover Submarine and Nancy Hank, the chairperson of the National Endowment of the Arts.

Entrepreneurship of individuals

It is entrepreneurship that is controlled and carried out by an individual or a family member with some personal motivations and initiatives, so it is referred to as individual entrepreneurship.

For instance, Steve Jobs, J.K Rolling, Mark Zukerberg, etc.

Entrepreneurship for Mass

The advent of this type of entrepreneurship happens when there is a presence among the popular masses of a lot of favorable atmosphere of encouragement and inspiration, and this defines mass entrepreneurship. It contributes to the development of a nation's small and large businesses.

Food caterers, beauty salons, and local shops are examples.

Small Entrepreneurship Company

Small firms recruiting more than 50 percent of the total non-governmental employees in the United States are more numerous in society. There is far less benefit in these kinds of businesses as the main reason behind them among employers is to make a living for their families.

Grocery shops, plumbers, confectionery stores, electricians, house cleaners, consultants, and hairdressers, among others, are some of the leading examples of small business entrepreneurship. By recruiting local people from family members, a small entrepreneur may be the individual who runs a company. The majority of them, by friends or family or business loans, finance their business.

Examples: Mint.com, core strength, Birchbox, and ozone coffee.

Big Entrepreneurship Company

As most of them expand using creativity, there are finite life cycles found in large businesses. Apart from the main products they make, this helps them to develop new versions. Customization of consumer demand, the establishment of new technologies, and the emergence of new rivals, among others, are the reasons for disruptive developments.

This contributes to the creation of entirely new products so that these problems can be effectively solved. This is achieved through major corporations, either by developing disruptive goods or by purchasing creative organizations. In large companies, technological innovation is very difficult to execute.

LG, Tata, Microsoft, and so on are several examples of big company entrepreneurship.

Scalable Entrepreneurship Startup

Most people assume that small businesses and Scalable Startup Entrepreneurship are similar. However, in fact, they are pretty different. The business starts with a vision that alters the world in this version of entrepreneurship. Support for such firms comes from venture capitalists, and that's why they hire top employees.

In this enterprise, the primary motive is to follow a flexible and repeatable business structure. They look for more funding after finding them so that businesses can expand. Because of risk participation, only a small number of companies are scalable startups.

Examples: websites for e-commerce, Facebook, etc.

Entrepreneurship in Social Relations

In this form of entrepreneurship, people in business are innovators who are concentrating on product and service creation in order to address social requirements and problems. In this scenario, the key motive of entrepreneurs is to change the environment, as opposed to scalable startup entrepreneurship.

SafePoint Trust is one of the premier examples of social entrepreneurship. It is managed by Marc Koska and is active in the redesign of medical instruments worldwide. In addition, they are introducing low-cost, non-reusable syringes for clinics that globally lack resources. This company has distributed more than 4 billion safe injections in more than 50 nations across the globe since its foundation.

Entrepreneurialism

Gifford Pinchot coined this word in the year 1973. It is focused on supporting entrepreneurs' activities in a broad company by enhancing the products and branding them to improve profitability. The valuable asset of an enterprise that the intrapreneur finds to be creative and committed efforts.

The four components of Intrapreneurship for a promising future are the right framework, adequate manpower, incentive, and cooperation. In this changing world of market competition, this entrepreneurship is very important.

E.g., Google, Intel, 3M, and so on are some examples of this kind of entrepreneurship.

Tecnopreneurship

It's a mixture of two phrases: technology and entrepreneurship. It is a kind of entrepreneurship in the sense of intensive technology and the process of combining entrepreneurial skills and technology in which technology is used as an integral component. It's a kind of new form of entrepreneurship and requires an innovative, techno-savvy, passionate entrepreneur as well as the ability to quantify the associated risk in advance.

Apple, Facebook, Twitter, Instagram, and so on are the most common examples of techno-partnership. IT plays an important role and provides advantages such as job generation, the best use of resources, technological development, and capital formation.

Entrepreneurship in Society

The cultural changes of these entrepreneurs who organize cultural, financial, social as well as human resources to make a profit out of it. They produce goods that are culturally good and that create a lot of economic, social, and cultural opportunities. These businesses are coming from micro, small to large companies.

Such entrepreneurship works with authors, writers, singers, dancers, marketers, bloggers, architects, and so on in cultural careers. The aim of such companies is to improve society through the leverage of industry. Cultural entrepreneurs often rely on media tools such as Twitter and Kickstarter to alter people's concepts, attitudes, and actions through contact and power.

Examples: singers, musicians, authors, artists.

Entrepreneurship of the International

It is the entire phase of advertising entrepreneurship, conducting the company's operations around the nation's borders. This includes numerous activities such as launching a company's new branches in new locations, exporting goods to other nations, acquiring a license to sell, and promoting products through nations. The aim of this entrepreneurship is to meet and satisfy the target audience's needs and wants.

As demand for goods rises globally, this entrepreneurship gets the advantage, but the need for the same product is not needed or decreasing domestically. It is very important in various ways, such as lower production costs, revenue and profit growth, globalization, cheap labor, the development of customer relationship management behaviors, and the use of talent and management skills to a large extent.

Examples: Google, Mcdonalds, Apple, etc.

Ecopreneurialism

It is called "Green entrepreneurship" as well. It includes the viewpoints that are through focusing on their targets as well as profitability signify companies with the environment. In the 1990s, this word gained prominence and was referred to as' environmental entrepreneurship.

This entrepreneurship, last but not least, is concerned with environmental concerns while concentrating on the business company's activities and its profit margin. Three key principles are used, such as Eco-innovation, Eco-opportunity, and Eco-commitment.

For instance: Body Shop and Ben and Jerry's, Patagonia, Clif Bars, Green Happiness Grow, etc.

Agripreneurship in Company

Agriculture has played a tremendous role in economic growth and its production as well. If a company owner has begun to make agricultural inventions, it is known as Agripreneurship. It is like a simple company that involves all of a business company's tasks, such as the cultivation, production, and distribution of farm supplies.

In addition to this, floriculture, horticulture, sericulture, animal husbandry, biotechnology, and so on are also included. Profitability, the use of digital technology to enhance agriculture, farm management, and creative solutions, and minimize crop waste are fundamentally a form of agricultural enterprise.

Examples of agri-partnership include Spin Cultivation, Rantachook, Herbal Processing Units, Plant Clinics, etc.

Transpreneurialism

When individuals from different gender groups such as transgender and Hijra come up with some small-scale companies to meet their everyday needs, it is commonly recognized as Transpreneruship. It is identified with the third gender class, where individuals are not only beggars or sex workers but also get their bread and butter from any small business.

For example: "Anam Prem" organized a fair in Mumbai where there were thirty-five stalls, and most of the shopkeepers belonging to transgender began their stalls of various products such as food, artificial jewelry, artificial flowers, and so on.

Entrepreneurship in Commerce

This form of entrepreneurship was only linked to profitability and stressed the possibilities and not the resources. It uses the tools available between the hierarchies and manages the network on the entity's behalf. It is seen as profit-based entrepreneurship as a big motive for all operations held by taking a profit. Around 250 years ago, this term was invented, and it focuses on the economy.

Examples: Any company that operates for profit, such as Tiktok, Facebook, Snapchat, and not for problems with society.

E- Entrepreneurialism

This is also known as Cyberpreneurship or E-Entrepreneurship. The sea of opportunities is where people, organizations as well as social and nations can use their cell phones and computer, again and again, to access the online services in this world full of technology. Every organization is already aware of the impact and outreach of the internet, and brick and mortar companies are less present.

Every business owner is trying to turn to online business and get a technology incentive. The word "Entrepreneurship" means that the bunch of resources is evaluated and defined and transformed into an online venture business the same. Also known as SENs, this kind of entrepreneur (Self Employed Entrepreneurs).

Examples include Amazon, eBay, Etsy, etc.

Inland Entrepreneurship

If a company owner creates products and offers services within a nation's borders, it is referred to as Domestic Entrepreneurship. In order to develop their company domestically, they obey all the rules and regulations relevant to the company defined by the country's government. It adheres to government policy, is highly convenient, culturally responsive, adapts technology, enhances awareness of the local system, increases development and risk opportunities, as well as incentives.

Examples include house cleaning, dog walking, freelance writing, etc.

Entrepreneurship Trading

They are a sort of mediator between a commodity maker and its consumers or distributors or wholesalers. Via such types of entrepreneurs, all the activities related to the trade of an enterprise are carried out. For distributors, wholesalers, suppliers, and consumers, it acts as intermediaries.

For instance: Paul Tudor Jones, Nick Leeson, John Key, etc.

Entrepreneurship from the Regime

If a business company is owned and controlled entirely by the state or state government, it is known as "State Entrepreneurship." All commerce, as well as industrial enterprises, is entirely conducted by the state alone, and there is not a single entrepreneur.

Examples: Any business focused on a state in India, such as Investpunjab.

Joint Entrepreneurialism

It is a private and public entrepreneurship partnership. If a corporation is jointly owned, operated, and run by a private businessman and the government, then it is called Joint Entrepreneurship.

Examples: Nokia and Microsoft Mobile Phone Innovations.

Chapter 2: 30 Ways to Become a More Successful Entrepreneur

Being successful also involves learning from others who have already accomplished their objectives. It is an amazing blessing for an entrepreneur to have a mentor, but not everyone can personally find one.

Here are 21 young or aspiring tips for entrepreneurs to help you get started if you have not found your personal business guru yet.

1. Challenge yourself.

His greatest inspiration, Richard Branson notes, is to continue to challenge himself. He treats life like a lengthy university education, where every day he will learn more. You, too, may!

2. Do some job that you care about.

There's no question that running a company takes a lot of time. Steve Jobs noted that doing work that you genuinely believe in is the only way to be happy in your life.

3. Take this chance.

When we are really doing it, we never realize the result of our efforts. It helped to realize that he would not regret failure, Jeff Bezos said, but he would regret not trying.

4. Have faith in yourself.

As Henry Ford famously said, "You're right, whether you think you can, or think you can't." Believe you can succeed, and you'll find ways across various barriers. You'll only make excuses if you don't.

5. Have a vision.

Tumblr's founder and CEO, David Karp, states that anyone who has a vision for something and a drive to create it is an entrepreneur. At all times, keep your vision open.

6. Select positive individuals.

Who you're with is who you're becoming. Reid Hoffman, the co-founder of LinkedIn, noted that hanging out with people who are already the way you want to be is the fastest way to improve yourself.

7. Face the anxieties.

It isn't easy to conquer fear, but it must be done. Once, Arianna Huffington said she found that fearlessness was like a muscle—the more she exercised it, the stronger it became.

8. Take action here.

The planet is filled with great ideas, but only by action can success come. Once, Walt Disney said the best way to get started is to stop talking and start doing it. For your performance as well, that's true.

9. Do it in time.

No one succeeds overnight, and everyone was a novice once. As Steve Jobs wisely observed, "If you look closely, it took a long time to achieve most overnight successes." Don't be afraid to spend time in your company.

10. Energy Management, not time.

What you can do with your time is limited by your energy, so manage it wisely.

11. Create a terrific squad.

In business alone, no one succeeds, and those who try will lose to a great team every time. To bolster your performance, create your own great team.

12. Character recruit.

Hire your character and beliefs as you develop your squad. You can always educate someone on skills, but after the fact, you can't make someone's values suit your company.

13. Capital raising scheme.

For upcoming entrepreneurs, Richard Harroch, a venture capitalist, has this advice: "It is almost always harder to raise capital than you thought it would be, and it always takes longer." So prepare yourself for that.

14. Know the priorities.

Ryan Allis, iContact's co-founder, pointed out that every day keeping the end in mind means you're working towards it. Set targets, and each day remind yourself of them.

15. Learn from errors.

As their best instructor, several entrepreneurs point to errors. You get closer to success as you learn from your failures — even though you initially struggled.

16. Know your client.

Dave Thomas, the founder of Wendy's, cited the client's awareness as one of his three keys to success. Know those that you represent better than anyone else, and you will be able to deliver the ideas you need.

17. Learn from grievances.

Bill Gates once said that it is the best source of learning for your most dissatisfied clients. Let disgruntled clients show you where the holes are in your operation.

18. Ask for the feedback of customers.

Thinking about what clients want or need will never contribute to achievement. You have to specifically question them and then carefully listen to what they're saying.

19. Spending wisely.

Be careful to spend it wisely while you are spending money on your business. Spending too much on foolish stuff is easy, and running out of money too fast.

20. Comprehend the industry.

Tony Hsieh, Zappos' founder, once said, "Don't play games that you don't understand, even if you see a lot of other people making money from them." The secret to success is to fully understand the business.

21. To deliver more than expected.

Larry Page of Google helps entrepreneurs to deliver more than clients expect. In your business, it's a perfect way to get noticed and create a loyal following of advocates.

It takes a lot of effort to be a good entrepreneur, a lot of vision, and a lot of perseverance. These 21 tips can help you walk the road far more easily, from entrepreneurs who have already found success.

2.1 Entrepreneurial Mindset: 5 Characteristics to Cultivate

Entrepreneurs help fuel economic growth, build opportunities, and develop goods or services that can make the world a better place. It takes outside-the-box thought and larger-than-life concepts to be a good entrepreneur. Anyone can come up with a creative concept, but the entrepreneurial challenge is creating a profitable company around it. The entrepreneurial mindset is distinctive in that to succeed but open to risk and failure; one must be imaginative, communicative, and highly motivated.

It's not just a big concept that paves the way for ultimate success in entrepreneurship. A company's success or failure is often due to the features of the creator himself. To combine one big idea into a fully functioning, the prosperous organization needs a specific aggregate of features. Is there a certain combination of abilities and characteristics that makes it possible for some entrepreneurs to be wildly successful?

It is enough to claim that in business, there is no secret recipe to succeed (if so, Harvard Business School would have patented it). There are, however, some features that should be cultivated by all aspiring entrepreneurs to significantly improve their own success chances. If you will, an entrepreneurial mentality will mark the difference between a lucrative company and one that shuts the doors before the first year is over.

So, what are these all-important characteristics that should be cultivated by aspiring or new entrepreneurs? What qualities seem to tip the scales in favor of a booming company is headed up? Read on as we share the views of our experts on the matter.

1. A Mental Optimistic Outlook

For entrepreneurs, why is a positive attitude important?

For successful entrepreneurs, a positive mindset and outlook is a must. For the rest of the company, the attitude of the company's headsets the stage and shapes organizational culture.

Negative thoughts hinder forward movement and the company's growth, not to mention the ability of management to direct managers and inspire employees. Positivity is part of what gives entrepreneurs the power to survive market downturns.

It's not a matter of sticking your head in the sand and avoiding anything that might go wrong to cultivate a positive outlook, but about learning how to mentally reframe your answer. In wallowing in errors, there is no point.

You will soon learn to develop a constructive approach to change by examining your reaction and response to a perceived problem. As a way to improve and learn, constructive individuals look at challenges, so you can try to concentrate on this ability.

For the overall work climate, why is positivity important? A positive mindset affects you in an equally positive way when you're the boss. Research shows that happier employees are better employees overall. A link between higher productivity and supportive working environments has been created by psychological studies. Moreover, higher company income, fewer sick days, and higher employee retention rates have been correlated with supportive work environments.

How Do You Maintain a Positive Mindset for Business?

Part of relinquishing negativity understands that creativity, time, and money are wasted by your own negative thoughts as a business leader.

Being optimistic is something which can be mastered, as all life skills. For the faint-hearted, being an entrepreneur is not. Both your personal life and mental attitude can be adversely influenced by the long hours and unpredictable demands of managing your own company.

Focusing on the things you can influence is one of the best ways to maintain a positive attitude. It is possible to track your health, amount of sleep, and ability to exercise. Each of these variables will assist you to remain concentrated, safe, and optimistic.

When you're working around the clock, where do you find time to make time for yourself? Research has shown that even a ten-minute walk every day will improve the mood and decrease the rate of negative thoughts.

2. An Attitude of Imaginative

For entrepreneurs, why is a creative mindset important?

Never was the adage "Creativity is the mother of invention" more true than in the business world. Think of the iPhone and Steve Jobs. Edison and a bulb of light. The Brothers Wright, and the plane. If it were not for healthy doses of imaginative gumption, each of these ground-breaking developments would not have come to fruition.

Even if you are not in an area that is "creative" for entrepreneurial success, innovation is required. An entrepreneur's mind is still searching for new thoughts and inventions. Any entrepreneurial product's basic life cycle stems from the conception of an idea, accompanied by converting the idea into a viable product or service.

The boss is the fact that you get to display creativity every day. To develop the organization and make improvements, you get to try out creative strategies. Even if you are not in a creative area, it is a creative act to figure out ways of improving your business operations per se.

You can apply innovative thinking to your sales, PR, recruiting, tech. The list is endless when you head up your own company.

How do you maintain an innovative market mindset?
Most entrepreneurs are innovative thinkers inherently; otherwise, they would not be able to take the creative leap to build their own business. That said, all of us should learn to be more inventive and tap into our innate talents.

There are ways to learn to develop your creative mind, whether or not you believe creativity is born to others or a learned trait. Visit The Creative Genius 'Entrepreneur's 5 Brain Training Strategies to learn how to develop and tap into your own creative mind.

3. Persuasive Capability for Contact

Why is it necessary for entrepreneurs to be persuasive?

Persuasive people are the greatest entrepreneurs. You can help bargain, close a deal, or score a lower price on your inventory with the power of persuasion. Not to mention, convincing individuals tend to be leaders who inspire, and they tend to be stellar managers.

How do you for the company cultivate persuasiveness?

Although certain individuals are more inherently persuasive than others, it is possible to learn and practice persuasive communication abilities. Learning to interact and present your ideas, no matter what your business is, will make you a stronger entrepreneur.

The differentiation between financial success or ruin may mean mastering convincing strategies. Here's how you can make the art of persuasion work in the business for you.

Reciprocating

Psychological research has shown that in business, the "reciprocity rule" can be very effective. The fundamentals of the rule in plain language are that when a person does you a favor, you must provide a favor in return. By "giving" something to the person you are trying to convince, try to make your convincing argument. You should either close the deal or make the order.

Look at the Others

The idea that individuals look to others for how to act in social settings is social evidence. In industry, social evidence can be used as a persuasive instrument. When you try to sell one of your items, it can help to make the sale to demonstrate how the product has been good for others.

Using Stickers

An effective persuasive tactic is to refer to one's credibility. By suggesting that they should behave in a manner that is compatible with a mark, you may use this mode of persuasion. For, e.g., say, "Your restaurant is a fine French restaurant, and our wine is stocked by good French restaurants." This is a common strategy used to generate sales in marketing campaigns.

4. Drive and Intrinsic Motivation

For entrepreneurs, why is intrinsic motivation important?

Intrinsic motivation is one of the top entrepreneurial attributes, meaning you are self-motivated as opposed to appealing to others to drive you to do something or keep you accountable. Broadly speaking, they are highly inspired to succeed by others who own their own companies. They poured blood, sweat, and tears into their company and may have literally mortgaged their future to open the doors of their companies first. Personally, getting a lot at stake drives the quest for inspiration.

How do you foster intrinsic business motivation?

Effective entrepreneurs realize that the secret to running a successful business is to remain motivated. What steps will you take to spark this inspiration and cultivate it?

Holding the emphasis on the endgame, the big picture, is one way to remain motivated in the long term. Where is your firm headed? What plans will you have in the future? How in the future will the business fit into its respective industry? Experts claim that the development of long-range strategies and plans keeps the fires of inspiration going.

Experts also advise, speaking of target setting, that goal setting is another way to keep the motivational wheels spinning. Setting high-quality objectives are the secret to user expectations for motivation.

What is that meant to mean? High-quality targets are essentially straightforward, achievable, and manageable. "This month, for instance, "I will attend two continuing education classes." Or "By Friday, I will recruit an editor for my company website." High-quality targets offer a sense of purpose when you reach your intended goal.

You're not only responsible for your own intrinsic motivation when you're the boss, but you are also responsible for fostering it for your staff. How do you inspire the workers to deliver the highest performance? For ways to empower and motivate the staff, visit our resource 10 Ways to Motivate Employees. With our tips, your staff will be inspired to give 100 percent to you and your company.

5. Tenacity and a learning ability from failure

For entrepreneurs, why is learning from mistakes serious?

When you launch a company, you hope your business will be a huge success. It's true that performance is great, but failure is where development and transformation occur. In fact, the secret to learning from failure is to learn and acknowledge your mistakes so that they make you stronger, not break you.

Don't be afraid to crash, because you'll be in good company when you do. At one time or another, the richest business owners, most decorated sports stars, and well-known musicians have all struggled in their journey to wealth and fame. Everyone is human, and therefore imperfect. In the pursuit of your business dream, do not consider yourself to be flawless. It is, by definition, unlikely.

How do you cultivate tenacity from failure in business and accept growth?

Loss is inevitable, but what you make of it is your response to your failure. Here's how to cultivate it and make use of your failure to excel in the long term.

Do not be afraid of the setback of your

When you fail, don't apply judgment or blame. Company loss does not cause you to feel humiliated or ashamed. Do your best to extract the emotions you create as an entrepreneur from mistakes so that you can objectively explore ways to develop yourself and your company. Turn off your negative self-talk and learn to tell, "Now for the next time I know better!" "Instead. Instead.

To learn from adversity, use Difficult Times.

Let adversity times lead you to power. Failure can be the best way for you to learn how to do things right. You will face many firsts as a startup new business owner and entrepreneur: first customer, first business lease, first employee hire. Some of these initials are not bound to work out; that's all right and planned. To build ideas and strategies about how you want to run your organization in the future, use these setbacks.

Share with others your experiences

It's human to fail at anything, which means that others forged that path before you. Share your thoughts with someone you trust to obtain some outside insight, whether it's your mentor, friends, or workers. Sharing your experience will help you work together to find an even better approach to how to deal with a tough issue in the future.

Don't be afraid of changing course and resetting.

Even the best-laid plans will go awry occasionally. That's both the essence of life and industry. There's going to be a moment when you might know something just doesn't work. You will have to change the direction you are preparing, reset, and start over.

Give Up Never!

Never giving up is one of the most critical keys to success in entrepreneurship. Perseverance is going to get you through those stressful times. To work for your goals, be tenacious. You'll accomplish them with persistence and grit; it just may not be overnight!

Completion

It could be the most exciting, fulfilling, the optimistic thing you have ever done to start your own business and run your own company. It can also be fraught with problems, self-doubt, and concerns. It's natural, that. You will create a prosperous company by learning how to adapt to the entrepreneurial mentality and develop key characteristics linked to success.

2.2 Entrepreneurial Traits for Career Success

Entrepreneurs assume all the risks of their companies, which can be a lot of pressure while rewarding. However, with the necessary entrepreneurial attributes, they are ideally placed to achieve their objectives. In this article, we address the nine characteristics that should be built for success by any entrepreneur.

What are the characteristics of entrepreneurship?

The traditional features, abilities, and thinking patterns associated with successful entrepreneurs are entrepreneurial characteristics. While some entrepreneurs are born with these characteristics, they can be created by others. They include:
- Being a competent leader
- Being upbeat
- Being trustworthy
- Being enthusiastic
- Disciplined Being
- Proactive being
- Maintaining an open mind
- Competitive being
- Being kind

1. Being a competent leader

It is expected that an entrepreneur can run a company, and most professionals in this role are also responsible for its startup. Entrepreneurship usually includes identifying and establishing investor relationships, managing staff, and controlling operations. You need to be an efficient leader in conducting these tasks well.

The desire to direct others is leadership. A productive leader mobilizes individuals to accomplish goals and is viewed by their followers as a leader. There are ways you can develop this attribute, such as:

Learning from your interactions

Although making mistakes while leading a team is normal, when you work and use your results to strengthen how you lead others, you can recognize the pros and cons of your leadership style.

Researching the various forms of leadership

For example, during the initial stage of setting up a company, the democratic style of leadership, which requires more cooperation between leaders and followers in the decision-making process, may be successful. If recruiting a large team of experts is not feasible, it can give an employer deeper insights into decision-making.

Learning about the leaders in your business

You will learn how business leaders monitor their main stakeholders and use the management techniques that work for your own company.

Developing a leadership strategy that works for you

You will find a leadership style that matches you and your organization by considering new forms of leadership and analyzing your leadership style.

2. Being upbeat

It is possible to characterize optimism as concentrating on the positive and becoming emotionally resilient to the negative. It is possible that an entrepreneur who organizes, manages, and runs an organization will face several setbacks over time. For starters, you will need to complete a lot of paperwork about permits, tax forms, business plans, and bank accounts when you start your business. There may be several challenges checking your progress in the process of having these documents ready, such as delays in getting a license or structural issues in your business plan.

Instead of being demotivated by them, being positive will help you rapidly solve these issues. Optimism is an attribute that you will need to build and retain in your career, like the other significant entrepreneurial traits. There are ways in which optimism can be cultivated, like:
- By recruiting cheerful staff, using positive quotes in your interior design, or listening to motivational music, fill yourself with optimism.
- Developing a positive perspective that affects the way you do things in your company and affects the decision-making process
- Starting to look at daily activities as opportunities for the company
- Identifying and concentrating on the good in a troublesome situation as you troubleshoot
- Finding a career coach who will help you create optimism

Catching yourself being pessimistic and reframing your outlook. For instance, as learning experiences that will prepare you for greater success in the future, you can begin looking at problems that check your progress.

3. Being trustworthy

Trust is a subjective conviction that for anything, you have what is necessary. Entrepreneurs ask banks for loans, recruit staff, inspire teams, and create consumer and supplier relationships, so it is important for an entrepreneur to be confident in their ability to do all these things well.

Being positive will assist your business. Key stakeholders, if you project your faith, are more likely to respond favorably to your proposals. To become more confident, you can use several strategies, such as:

- Cultivate trust in you and your skills. Create a list of your achievements in times of uncertainty and remind yourself of them. Remind yourself, for instance, that you are making something that customers want to buy or recall the things you have already done to make your company more successful.
- Plan and carry out your everyday tasks with the mentality that, even though there are failures, you can successfully complete them.
- Research how trust can be expressed by body language and verbal communication and use these tools to strengthen the way you project yourself.
- Role-play scenarios such as deals with key suppliers or investor meetings by practicing the delivery of your post, learning to answer common questions, and professionally managing input.
- Hire a career coach who will assist you in building your confidence.
- Spend time with friends who have a beneficial influence on the way you feel about yourself. Such social interactions will amplify your confidence.
- To boost your job efficiency, learn new hard, and soft skills. This will motivate you at work and become more self-assured.
- Make improvements that will enhance your appearance to improve your morale, such as dressing well, exercising regularly, and eating healthily.

4. Being enthusiastic

Being passionate about building and running your company will make it easier for a successful business to put in the effort necessary. Consider these tips if you need to improve your professional passion

Try to think of your work as more than just a means of survival and grow a real passion for what you do. You can recall why you wanted to start your own business or think about the positive influence your company has on yourself, your workers, your customers, or your society.

Start the business day by recalling all the things you're looking forward to doing, such as concluding a contract or recruiting a new employee.

When you engage with colleagues, vendors, or customers, learn how to express your passion. Your passion for what you're doing is also going to make your major stakeholders feel more excited, which could assist your business.

5. Disciplined Being

Being disciplined will assist you as an entrepreneur to achieve success. It is predicted that entrepreneurs will work individually, set their own goals, and resolve setbacks.

Being disciplined is important for doing these things well. To become more disciplined, you can use the following advice:
- Train yourself to be a self-starter who, without the need for supervision, initiates, and completes tasks.
- The time you meet a target, give yourself a small reward. Without being distracted, this will help you to achieve your goals.
- Create a work ethic that drives your commitment to work hard to accomplish your professional objectives. Bear in mind that more time has been spent at work by many entrepreneurs who have created successful startups than any of their workers.

6. Proactive being

A proactive person anticipates and attempts to resolve opportunities and challenges, while a reactive person responds simply to circumstances. As an entrepreneur, instead of being reactive, it is often easier to be constructive. Here are several ways you can make yourself more proactive:
- To consider the needs of key stakeholders, combine analysis with active listening to (your customers, employers, and business partners).
- Before these problems become more serious, recognize risks in incidents, and establish solutions.
- Regularly analyze your business processes. Identify and strengthen the areas that can be strengthened.
- Instead of developing short-term strategies that are unsuccessful, aim to develop long-term solutions to resolve the principal causes of problems.
- To show workers that you appreciate their input, use verbal and written correspondence. This will assist you in finding areas that need to be changed or procedures that need to be more clearly communicated to employees.

7. Maintaining an open mind

Keeping an open mind requires the ability to listen to others' viewpoints and ideas. Entrepreneurs usually start companies in competitive sectors that have already established market leaders. To succeed in this role, in daily events, it is important to see business opportunities and look for ways to enhance business offerings. Consider the following tips to improve this trait:
- Instead of refusing to agree that someone else may have a valuable opinion, be willing to listen to others. This will improve your reservoir of thoughts and perspectives.
- Encourage peers or clients to provide input and consider their views in order to enhance a product or service.
- To enhance a product or service offering, use fresh ideas or observations about workflows, customer service, or employee engagement.

8. Competitive being

Among successful entrepreneurs, competition is a key trait. Industries are growing more dynamic with globalization and virtualization. It is important to cultivate a competitive attitude to sustain a lucrative market. To improve your competitiveness, consider the following advice:
- Keep track of what the competitors do with market research and market monitoring services, and make sure that in terms of development, you do not fall behind.
- Identify the market strategies that work for your rivals as well as those that do not work, and use these strategies to boost your organization.
- To make your products more competitive in the market, use product enhancements, pricing, marketing, and distribution. In a market with several established brands, for example, you can price a new product at a relatively low price and invest in creative advertising to motivate customers to switch brands and try your product.
- Develop client assessments and use your findings to continue improving your products or services by making them more customer-friendly.
- To recruit the best talent to your team, use employee research to create compensation such as benefits, severance packages, and performance-based rewards.

9. Being kind

While kindness is not generally seen as an essential characteristic of entrepreneurs, it can enable you to sustain success. For instance, although it is easy to concentrate on reaching your KPIs on sales, failing to consider your employees' well-being or overlooking the effect of a production process on your community may cause you problems over time or allow your competitors to gain an advantage. To cultivate kindness, you can use the following tips:
- Regularly assess your full-time employees' working conditions and ensure that they have the basics they need to perform well.
- Re-evaluate your employment benefits on a regular basis to ensure that you have a package that will genuinely help employees and retain the best talent.
- To make them less damaging to the environment and more sustainable, be proactive in improving your manufacturing or distribution processes.
- Strong policies that discourage bullying, sexual harassment, or gender-based discrimination promote supportive, healthy company culture.

2.3 Characteristics of an Entrepreneur

It takes particular skills to be an entrepreneur. Although some skills might naturally be present, with diligent practice, others can be learned or established. Understanding the qualities that entrepreneurs need will help you grow to become a better leader in business. In this article, we clarify 15 characteristics of entrepreneurs that can be improved.

What are the qualities of an entrepreneur?

The attributes of entrepreneurs are qualities that help entrepreneurs achieve their goals. An entrepreneur is someone who produces, organizes, and runs their own company. Entrepreneurs include examples of:

Online business owners: Online business owners include bloggers, e-commerce, or any business owner who conducts mainly online business activities.

Home-based business owners: As opposed to offices, home-based entrepreneurs operate their business from their home.

Inventors: Inventors are entrepreneurs who develop and sell their inventions on the market.

Entrepreneurship, in any situation, means innovating new concepts, bringing them into action, and persevering through obstacles. Some entrepreneurial characteristics are inherent personality attributes, but you can cultivate skills and characteristics through practice as well.

The entrepreneur features you can make.

To become a better entrepreneur, here are 15 characteristics you should improve:
- Creativeness
- Love
- Encouragement
- Connaissance of good or service
- Networking Skill
- Self-assurance
- Optimism
- Vision for
- Mindset on Goal
- Take chances
- Persuasive
- Decision-and Making
- Tenaciousness
- Management of Capital

Entrepreneurship

- Customisability

1. Creativeness

To become an entrepreneur begins with an idea. You need to see possibilities, find innovative ways to do things, and provide the public with solutions.

Develop habits that help the creative system in order to boost your creativity. Think about what makes you feel innovative, like music, people meeting, reading, or some other activity. To find inspiration for creative solutions, devote a special part of your day. Start by doing what inspires you throughout this part of the day, then let your mind flow. You should make a list of thoughts and choose those to try.

2. Love

What drives entrepreneurs is passion. Typically, they enjoy what they do, and this allows them to spend their time on their projects.

Reflect on the significance of your job in order to become a more passionate entrepreneur. Remember that you are helping to find solutions that will help many individuals. Knowing that your dedication has an effect will give you the motivation you need to continue when there is uncertainty or when it becomes challenging for the organization. What keeps you focused on your target is love.

3. Encouragement

The will to do such things is motivation. Businesspeople are motivated to make their company successful and push themselves.

You can begin by setting small targets in order to increase motivation. Small targets will help you accomplish bigger goals and inspire you to reach higher. Recognize the work already done and, even small ones, enjoy the performance. Often, cultivate a good outlook. In order to concentrate on what you want to do and the positive aspects of your life, turn your attention away from negativity and everyday obstacles.

4. Connaissance of good or service

Entrepreneurs understand what they have to sell and to whom it can be offered. Identify explicitly the type of goods or services you sell and how they provide customers with value. Study your target customers, too, to ensure that you respond to their needs. This will encourage you to continually enhance your offer so that you can remain on top of industry trends.

You should constantly learn about your business, understand what consumers need, and know the characteristics that separate you from rivals in order to maximize the positive impact of this information. Speak and use their suggestions for the customers. You can change your location with this information when appropriate.

5. Networking Skill

For good entrepreneurship, the ability to communicate with people and to identify opportunities for collaboration is crucial. Meeting new people might make it easier to access the resources or information your company requires. It enables you to benefit from others' performance, to promote your services or products, and to reach new customers.

You must strive to develop sincere relationships to strengthen your networking skills. You obviously have a business purpose in mind; however, just like making new friends, approach people with the intention of a human connection. Link them if you encounter someone who might be of interest to another person in your network. Not only are you going to help someone, but they're definitely going to remember you, and they're going to want to return the favor.

6. Self-assurance

Entrepreneurs assume that they can accomplish their objectives. They may be in doubt, but through it, they persevere. They are prepared to invest in the work they need because they are assured that something better than what already exists can be produced.

Self-confidence is vital because it makes it easier for you to feel better and to resolve obstacles, take chances, and be resilient. It also leads overall to your performance.

You may use the visualization approach to increase your self-confidence. Visualize yourself as the individual you want to be and visualize your organization at a point you'd be proud of. By saying uplifting remarks about your successes, you can also practice encouragement. These strategies will help to modify the way you positively see yourself.

7. Optimism

With a strategy in motion, entrepreneurs are dreamers: they see the bright side of the situation and still step forward. Optimism promotes innovation because it inspires business owners to find fresh ideas for their goods or services and improves their chances of success.

To build your confidence, instead of issues that might stop you, you should see obstacles as opportunities to learn. Keep in mind the end target, and don't concentrate on past problems.

8. Vision for

Businessmen have a vision. They see a larger vision that they want to achieve, fueling their efforts, and motivating them to do more. Vision, however, is what determines an organization's culture and identity. It not only keeps entrepreneurs energized, but it helps them to encourage others and keep them working for the success of the business.

You should execute a regular action plan to boost your entrepreneurship vision. It will prevent you from feeling stressed and help you stick to your vision by prioritizing your tasks. Also, to reinforce your mind, and remain focused on your goal, listen to or read uplifting material.

9. Mindset on Goal

Entrepreneurs are geared toward goals. They know what they want to accomplish, set an aim, and work towards that goal. To resolve potential obstacles, persistence is important, and it also encourages trust from the people who work with you.

To become more goal-oriented, you can start by outlining what you want to achieve and clarifying your vision of the future. Then, set a goal to direct your acts with a timeline. This will allow you to witness your success and help keep you committed to your objective.

10. Take chances

Entrepreneurs are primed for risk-taking. They prepare for the unexpected so that measured choices can be made that are profitable for them and their business.

You should begin to view your path as a learning process, including potential setbacks, in order to increase your risk-taking skills. You must bear in mind your target and commit to perseverance.

To distinguish from your competition and allow your company to succeed, it is vital to take some risks. You can become more comfortable with challenging yourself until you know how you can handle the danger and learn from disappointments.

11. Persuasive

Entrepreneurs know their organization and how to communicate with individuals about it. To believe in their theory, they need to convince others.

Learn about your listeners and adjust to their personalities to develop your persuasive skills. In order to meet them on an emotional level and demonstrate your passion, you should share a story. It creates a bond that can develop into loyalty if people can relate to your story, which is important for your business success. To help your points and persuade others, another piece of advice is to share your successes and rely on evidence.

12. Decision-and Making

For the success of their company, entrepreneurs need to make fast decisions and take action.

You should educate yourself to better understand the issues you are trying to address in order to develop your decision-making skills. Consider the effect of the decision that you need to make and give a reasonable period of time to decide. To ease the process of making a decision, you can also limit your choices.

13. Tenaciousness

Challenges are solved by entrepreneurs. They persevere and hold on to their objectives and dreams despite difficulties.

You should write down your priorities and read them every day to strengthen your tenacity. You may pick role models and recall great historical figures who had to persevere before they achieved success through failure.

14. Management of Capital

Entrepreneurs need to consider their company's financial condition. Even if they employ a professional like an accountant, they are the decision-maker and have to understand their situation to effectively run the company.

By making a budget and sticking to it, and saving available funds rather than wasting them, you will strengthen your basic money management skills. By taking courses or training programs, you can also learn more financial information.

15. Customisability

Entrepreneurs also need to multitask when they begin a venture. In difficult circumstances, flexibility in your schedule, as well as in your thinking, is essential to continue rising.

You should approach all tasks with an open mind to improve your adaptability and, if necessary, remain ready to change your ways. To encourage your ability to adapt, try new approaches, and accept new trends.

Chapter 3: Powerful Ways for Entrepreneurs to Be More Creative

There will be times when the mind simply goes blank, not finding a creative thought. There are times when even experts lose their creative genius. Your creativity declines as your age mature unless you proactively nurture it and strive on a daily basis to be more creative.

It may be from stress accumulation or from being incredibly busy when your creativity seems to disappear entirely. You may try to fix a problem, and you may not be able to visualize a good solution. It can be very hard to pull yourself out and start getting more creative again when momentarily stumped.

You will motivate yourself to create more new ideas and ultimately solve your problem in many ways, but sometimes you have to force yourself to discover new and unique ways to get back your creativity. As an entrepreneur, there's no other option if you hope to become successful in the business world.

Here are strong ways in which entrepreneurs can be more creative. They won't all work for you, but it shouldn't take very long to get your creativity flowing again if you test out some of these tactics:

1. Collecting new ideas and resources

At all times, be on the lookout for new ideas and inspiration within your areas of interest. Widely read. Using the internet as a medium for learning. Take an interest in what's going on around you in the industry. Keep in your browser or in your inbox a bookmark folder containing anything you find interesting that you think you might refer to again. This is a fund you can tap on rainy days whenever you need some creative inspiration.

2. Moving to another Operation

Our best thoughts always come when we don't even know we're thinking about a problem. Your mind will continue to work on the issue you left behind subconsciously if you move on to another activity. How many times have you tried to remember something frustratingly given up, only for the missing thought to pop back into your head later when you were least expecting it? Embrace this subconscious process of creation and let it become a major part of your workflow.

3. Brainstorming Over

A highly productive way to come up with new innovative ideas can be brainstorming. By writing your general issue in the middle of the page, combine this with a mind map. Think of some very general areas to work on from there, drawing these from the central idea as offshoots. Branch out further from these outshoots and until you've begun to find what you're looking for, continue to break down ideas into more digestible bits.

4. Brainstorm Reverse

Instead of concentrating solely on the possible solutions, reverse brainstorming can help identify possible causes of issues. You try to brainstorm real problems, rather than solutions, with this form. You may find new approaches to solving problems by addressing issues in this way.

5. Shift adverse ideas into a positive mindset

It will encourage you to be more innovative simply by shifting your attitude. "Ask yourself, "I can work out this" or "I'm open to any thoughts someone can come up with." You are much more likely to get a rush of creative inspiration by repeating these positive thoughts that will help you solve your problem and far less likely to throw away possible solutions that come to mind.

6. Dream of Memories of Nice

You do not have to limit the constructive thoughts to just the issue at hand. It would be much easier for you to come up with ideas by looking back to creative achievements and happier memories in the past.

7. Meditate by yourself

Increased concentration, patience, calmness, clarity, perspective, and insight include some of the advantages of meditation. Improving all of these can greatly boost creativity levels.

8. Clarify your principles

We all obey whether we know it or not, a personal collection of principles. As we age, we build our belief system, and that's very much how we look at life and the world around us. In order to reflect on your values, take time. The act of examining your personal value system will help develop new ideas.

9. From the Mundane, take a break

For a day, break your routine. Do stuff differently. Change your way of going to work. Meet the new guys. Eat new foodstuffs. Do a thing that you have never done before, just for a day to be different. It is likely the "new you" will come up with new ideas.

10. Be a Perfectionist, stop

Perfectionists spend a lot of time trying to get the info right that they rarely take time outside of their comfort zones to think creatively about new solutions. Your brain has no room left for creative thinking if you worry about perfectionism. Before sharing it and working to improve it, don't wait until an idea is fully formed.

11. Watch a video of Stimulating

TED discussions are an obvious place to start, but on YouTube, there are also several videos that are sure to get the creative juices flowing. Only stop allowing yourself to get distracted by cute cats' posts.

12. Read Biographies of Inspiring, Talented People or Autobiographies

Reading about other effective and creative people is another way to stimulate the brain. Just by reading about what worked for brilliant minds in the past, you will pick up a great deal. How have they been solving their problems with creativity? Is there anything from their achievements or mistakes that you can learn?

13. Determine the goals

Think about your long-term goals and break them down into results of shorter-term action. This will send the mind into a creative mode and make what you should and shouldn't concentrate on perfectly clear.

14. Start a Journal

It will help you unlock some serious imagination by writing in a journal. It's a perfect way to come across new ideas when they pop into your mind if you allow yourself the chance to focus on the success of the day and type down the issues you're facing.

15. Listen to a podcast

The podcast of Tim Ferriss is especially great for improving creativity because he brings on some of the world's most experienced, talented, and imaginative minds. Listen to Tim's interview with James Altucher, for instance, and you will not regret it.

16. Stimulate different regions of the brain

If you're struggling to use one area of your brain to be innovative, try to switch to another, even if it's not an area you're traditionally strong in. If you struggle in a conversation to come up with a solution to your problem, try to imagine a solution to your problem, or maybe you should go through the physical phase of creating a model.

17. Draw a picture

For those who are more visually inclined, one especially good type of inspiration is to draw an image. What you're beginning to draw doesn't matter too much. It can grow spontaneously and follow an entirely unexpected course. With the acceptance that the end result is not as relevant as the process of actually taking time to doodle, go into your drawing session.

18. Adjust your surroundings physically

To inspire the brain to come up with fresh ideas and new concepts get more creative again, a change of scenery can be all you need. Take a day trip to a place where your senses can be enhanced, go down to a local park, or go for a stroll and find a new place to do some work without someplace in mind beforehand.

19. Surrounding yourself with nature

Many people think that just by being present outside, they get a creative jolt. Fresh air, chirping birds, sunlight, and other natural scenes to take in is typically a good change of pace, especially for a business person living in the area.

20. Green or Blue Go

It's not always possible to reach the countryside physically, particularly if you live in a major city. Some of the advantages of this can, however, be obtained by simply being in a green or blue area. Such colors are assumed to help comprehension and decrease uncertainty. Surround yourself with bright colors, such as in a flower garden or an art gallery, if you are seeking even more imaginative, original thoughts.

21. Organize your personal room and Declutter it

There are whole websites dedicated to your life being decluttered. Many decluttering proponents claim that you can declutter your mind by decluttering your life.

22. Get active by exercising and moving

Working out activates the brain in the hippocampus zone, producing new neurons. Physical exercise can trigger new, innovative thinking habits, such as going for a run, taking a stroll around the city, practicing yoga, or even doing some pushups and sit-ups. As a way to withdraw from work and gain greater motivation, many individuals use their workout time.

23. Emphasis on exercises with breathing

Breathing exercises might not be as energetic as most other styles of exercise, but they may help you relax just as well. Aware breathing exercises will assist you to concentrate on your main goals when you find yourself straying away.

24. Have a massage

A massage will help place you in such a relaxed headspace that fresh new ideas are more likely to catch you.

25. Let Daydream about Yourself

If you are not completely centered all the time, don't feel bad. Daydreams also lead to flashes of strange insight. If you feel like you really need it, encourage your mind to wander. Just make sure you have a handy notepad to document any new ideas, regardless of whether they are specifically connected to the issue at hand or not.

26. Consult with someone you know

You don't need to separate yourself if you're in a creative rut. If you and other individuals bounce ideas around, some of these things, such as brainstorming, work very well, and you're likely to get some of the best new ideas from getting opinions from others who think differently than you.

27. Call a Member of Friend or Family

Often, even though it's totally off subject, actually talking to a good friend or family member will help alleviate tension that prevents you from finding the answers You're searching for.

28. Take a (Short) Bar Trip

To jumpstart your creative thinking process again, a drink at your local bar will calm you enough, and people watching while doing so might be even more beneficial.

29. Got Family Time

It is possible that spending time with your family will decrease your stress levels and hopefully give you more resources to put into your creative thinking.

30. Listen to Music Relaxing

The deep links between listening to music and creative thinking have been shown by several studies. There are, of course, many styles of music, some more conducive than others to creative thinking. Pick something calming in the background that can play.

31. Watching a game

To help generate new ideas, there are quite a few games you can play. Build a game for a meeting where everybody gets to play and has the chance to propose fresh ideas. They'll have a real opportunity to push themselves to propose new out-of-the-box suggestions if people find the activity enjoyable.

32. Go to a video

Take a break from the movies, and for a few hours, shut your mind down from work. Don't feel bad about that issue. When you return to your career, it will probably be with a renewed emphasis.

33. Stop intentionally during the middle of a project

Similar to Ernest Hemingway's approach to warding off the block of the writer by ending his writing sessions with stopping mid-sentence, it can be equally successful to consciously take a break from unfinished ventures. It can have enormous advantages to give your mind the chance to think about the issue when you are relaxing and doing other things.

34. Go Early to Bed Early

You are likely to be refreshed with a few extra hours of sleep, and you might very well wake up tomorrow with new ideas.

Ultimate Thoughts

Not every solution will work for everyone, but the strategies that leave you mentally refreshed will be identified. For entrepreneurs, this means new ideas, motivation, and wisdom that can revitalize your business's success. Don't feel guilty in the short term for taking time away from your company because a much-improved state of mind will be the product of properly nursing your imagination.

3.1 Role and Importance of Entrepreneurship

The Entrepreneur, who boosts the economy and rejuvenates the existing business companies that sustain an economy's structure, is the key to the establishment of a new company. Under the headings below, the role of entrepreneurship in the growth of a nation's economy is clarified. Let's take a look at the following ones below.

1. Fresh Development of Work

Entrepreneurship businesses all over the world generate a significant share of jobs. They offer lots of entry-level jobs that allow the unqualified employees to obtain training and the requisite experience.

In fact, a large portion of employment is generated annually by small businesses. That's not all; they build and provide large-scale enterprises with skilled staff.

2. Creation of societies

If the job base is split into lots of small entrepreneurial enterprises, a group can work very beautifully. It aims to raise hygiene standards and improves homeownership at the highest level.

Additionally, it will provide the group with extra stability and a better quality of life.

3. Nationwide Sales

Do you know that entrepreneurial enterprises create a great kind of wealth? There is no question that current companies are leaders in current markets. The entrepreneurial firms, however, are still not far behind, as they are the ones that offer the nation new money.

4. Boosts Living Standard

If you don't know, living standards are measured on the basis of a household's consumption of goods and services at a given time. The existence of diversified units depends greatly on it.

So, entrepreneurship offers great kinds of goods. On top of that, they raise the wages of people working for them.

5. Promotes growth & research

Innovation is the main cornerstone of entrepreneurship, as we all know, and that's why you're going to see entrepreneurs with lots of new ideas that they test through experiments.

The thing that we want to say is that entrepreneurship generates funds for research & growth. In simple words, it is boosted by things such as general growth and science.

6. Self-Independence

Entrepreneurs have become one of the world's principal corner stores of self-reliance. The explanation behind this is that they help build wonderful replacements for imported units that reduce reliance on other nations.

In addition, it gives nations the opportunity to export to foreign countries goods and solutions that allow them to gain national exchange. We want to say, in clear terms, that economic independence is assured by entrepreneurs.

7. Expanding established companies

Entrepreneurship plays a great role in boosting a company's creativity, growth, and expansion.

Entrepreneurs are making the requisite efforts to increase the number of units in their current businesses. In addition, it helps to improve current manufacturing strategies to extend the network across the globe.

8. Formation Of Capital

Via industrial security concerns, entrepreneurs can mobilize public savings. If public savings have been invested in the sectors, national resources are optimally utilized. Since the rate of capital accumulation that is required for rapid economic growth is tilting, this is the reason that the maker of wealth is an entrepreneur.

9. Make changes to Per Capita Income

An Entrepreneur creates opportunities and locates them. In the form of goods and services, all latent wealth, as well as idle resources such as land, labor, and savings, have been transformed into national income. Maximizing the national product and per capita income of a country, which is the benchmark for measuring economic development, is absolutely critical.

10. Opportunities pool

An Entrepreneur creates job opportunities directly and indirectly at all times. Directly creating a company and working to live an honorable life as an independent entrepreneur. On the other hand, by starting a large and small business company, they give people millions of jobs. It thus reduces the nation's unemployment problem and also provides for individual growth.

11. Developing the areas

These public and private companies easily reduce regional inequalities in order to create an economic development balance. They set up factories in remote areas to benefit from different concessions as well as subsidies, as offered by a nation's central and state government.

12. Improving living standards

Some goods and products that are important are often introduced by an entrepreneur, but their availability is limited. The mass production of goods and the production of handicrafts in the countryside by small-scale factories helps to raise the quality of life of an average citizen. Not only the availability of the goods required, but it also provides the same at a pocket-friendly price and increases the differences in consumption.

13. Democracy in Economic Affairs

In national self-reliance, entrepreneurship plays an important part. Industrialists often make efforts to create countless replacements for items previously imported, thus helping to reduce the reliance on other foreign nations on commodities. These products are also exported to other countries and help countries increase their foreign exchange for the nation. On the one hand, export promotion and import substitution on the other side ensure that the reliance on other nations is minimized.

14. Multiple linkages

When an industry is created to manufacture such goods, because of the demand for raw materials, it has a chain response. There are many backward and forward linkages to the start of a business enterprise. The start-up of a steel plant generates various ancillaries to demonstrate this, thereby increasing the market for iron ore, coal, and so on.

These are backward links supplied by Entrepreneurs. It encourages the growth of m,machine-building, the production of utensils, and some other units by optimizing the steel supply.

Entrepreneurship

15. Wealth and sharing formation

By beginning a business, an entrepreneur invests his own money and receives capital from investors and lenders in the form of debt and equity. In addition, they use public funds to encourage people to recognize lucrative deals as their money rises with company growth. It is useful for the production and distribution of resources for the sake of economic growth.

16. Demand from Customers

Entrepreneurs manufacture a wide variety of goods according to people's tastes and demands. They satisfy the demand of customers without any shortage of goods and let them buy what they are looking for. Thus, all consumer demands are fulfilled within the country, and the export of foreign products is reduced.

17. Social advantage

They inspire democracy and self-governance alike. In addition, they help to reduce the extent of social issues such as lack of work opportunities, low living standards, self-dependence, etc. It is a good way to equitably allocate the national income among the members of society.

18. Growth Capital Market

The basis for starting up a company is an investment. An Entrepreneur raises funds from investors as well as financial agencies for investment in the company. The public is engaged in exchanging shares and debentures with certain financial suppliers, contributing to capital market growth.

19. The Development of Infrastructure

A nation's economic growth relies on the development of infrastructure. Entrepreneurs are still in support of rising backward and rural areas that strive to use capital and create job opportunities as well. They demand that the government improve the infrastructure of the region in order to develop business in those areas.

20. Creation for Traders

Entrepreneurs have played an undeniable part in the development and promotion of both domestic and international trade. In the form of trade credit, overdraft, cash credit, secured loans, unsecured loans, and short-term loans, various financial institutions assist. These investment funds are contributing to the growth of trade across the country.

21. Integration of Economics

The power to generate employment opportunities is not in few hands by setting up different business projects across the regions of the country. As framed by the concerned government, Entrepreneur adopts various economic policies as well as laws related to the industry. By following the same rules for the effective functioning of business operations in the country, the gap between the rich and the poor is reduced.

22. Raise Money Abroad

In addition to receiving funds from domestic investors, entrepreneurs often receive their investments from individuals and institutions based in foreign countries. In this way, the influx of foreign capital into the nation increases and results in economic growth.

23. Promotion to Export

The goods manufactured by a corporation are not supplied to a nation's people, but they are also exported globally. It thus decreases the burden of a nation's balance of payment by exporting its goods. In addition, they receive some foreign exchange in the country as well.

24. Innovative approaches to problems

In order to deal with a nation's familiar issues, the organization engaged in the field concerned often attempts to find a new approach. The new methods that were not used before can be tried by an entrepreneur, and this is a highlighted argument that contributes to a nation's economic growth. In the form of services or products, the solution to such problems might be.

To demonstrate, Paytm's amazing move is the best example of digitalizing transactions when demonetization took place in India, and people were unable to make critical transactions due to lack of cash.

25. Send others inspiration

The development of a business offers other individuals a chance to get involved in the Entrepreneurial venture and gain valuable experience. This helps other colleagues and workers to start a company and produce some creative goods and services for the good of the economy. The inspiring method leads to the growth of a chain response and contributes to the economy by improving healthier entrepreneurial practices.

26. Growth of production techniques

Over the past few decades, different traditional methods of manufacturing and producing a commodity have been used. But there is some promotion of new techniques that use fewer resources and produce more advantages with the creation of new entrepreneurial activities across nations. It lowers manufacturing costs and results in budget-friendly goods with comparable results. The introduction of creative technology has a beneficial effect on a nation's economy.

27. Ambassador for Social Transition

Entrepreneurs serve as ambassadors in an economy by encouraging innovative and creative innovations. All of the inventions give people a cultivated scientific look and help them leave the traditional views and ideas behind.

28. Strengthen an economy's human development index

Entrepreneurs often affect a nation's people and help them to engage in new practices and innovations. It provides individuals with many resources and helps them to upgrade their skills by embracing and using emerging technology. It helps in human resource growth and has a positive effect on a nation's Human Development Index.

Up Wrapping

Depending on the availability of capital, the environment of business, and how sensitive the political system is, the role and value of entrepreneurship in economic growth vary from time to time. Entrepreneurs have made more investments in advantageous situations relative to nations with unfavorable conditions of opportunity.

It is crystal clear that entrepreneurship serves as a catalyst for the growth of the economy of the country.

3.2 Why Creativity is so Crucial for Entrepreneurs?

Entrepreneurial phase characteristics

Entrepreneurship is like doing every other business, but there are some aspects that differentiate it from conventional methods of business.

Creativity

The mind of an entrepreneur revolves around creative ideas and create opportunities. In order to find niches and take the risks of entering them, there is a constant and conscious effort needed. Entrepreneurship includes the ongoing review of current business workflows and the discovery of ways to carry them out in terms of time and expense in a more productive and effective way. In simple terms, entrepreneurship operates towards market optimization.

Economic significance

In order to create effective processes, entrepreneurship works towards maximizing resources and making good use of them. By growing the economic activity that entails improving the entire operation, increases the wealth of a business, and adds profit.

More Gain

The entrepreneurship method rewards the employee by growing the enterprise's profit potential. This is the outcome of new ideas being undertaken and an innovative product or service being delivered.

Risk-Taking

Entrepreneurship's entire nature revolves around the confidence and capacity to take new risks. To observe an idea's fruitful consequence, patience is required, and it takes time and effort to go from conceptualization to idea implementation. This moment and commitment is the chance the Entrepreneur is prepared to take.

Work Prospects

Entrepreneurship, which needs a workforce, generates new niches and businesses. For young people, this offers exciting career prospects. Therefore, with creativity and profit, entrepreneurship has tremendous job creation potential.

The method of entrepreneurialism

The entrepreneurial process begins with an idea's creation and refinement, accompanied by implementation and management.

For entrepreneurs, why is innovation so crucial?

A detailed observation of the entrepreneurial process reveals that innovative thinking is an entrepreneur's must-have "skill" to develop new ideas. Creativity helps a person to invent interesting processes, which gives entrepreneurs so many benefits.

But what exactly makes innovation in the work-life of an entrepreneur so critical and important?

Creativity contributes to performance through:

Creating new strategies for competitive advantage. The entire entrepreneurship process is rooted in new concepts being developed and explored. It gives him an advantage over the competition when an entrepreneur is able to produce a new concept that is feasible as well as successful. The ability to explore various niches is just like a skill gained or a person-possessed resource.

Thinking of new ways to grow your brand and enhance the business. Creativity helps to create new ways to enhance an existing product or service and to optimize a business. The deliverables of an organization still have a scope for improvement; it is the innovative Entrepreneur who can decide how to do it.

Thinking the impossible. To create the most obscure ideas, creativity involves imagination. To cross the boundaries of "usual" and "normal" or to think outside the box, creativity is needed. This encourages entrepreneurs to think beyond conventional strategies, to come up with something new, interesting, scalable, and yet to have the potential for success.

Finding similar patterns in various fields. Often the thought process often goes along the line of those existing processes due to following a routine or a habit. Creativity helps individuals to connect diverse and unrelated subjects and generate good ideas for entrepreneurship. The fusion of multiple fields produces fascinating intersections, creating new niches. Most individuals are afraid of putting together different disciplines, but the fascinating concepts come from various fields that overlap.

By innovation and entrepreneurship, creating new niches. It is critical that new facets of traditional business are explored in entrepreneurship. This may be in the form of changing the way the product is made, or the service is provided, or how it is delivered to the customer. All these fields can build a gap in business that has great potential.

How are they linked? Entrepreneurship and Innovation

We have now evaluated the entrepreneurs who are willing to attribute innovation to their success. But what connects entrepreneurship and innovation exactly?
The creative mind and the business mind are connected by entrepreneurs.

In today's world, goods are produced and exported to foreign markets due to globalization and excessive industrialization. As a consequence, access to any commodity, anywhere, is easier. The customer has access to different types of goods that vary in type and quality. So in a market filled with goods, what does a business person do? In markets where consumers already have their expectations and preferences that are trusted, too many options to choose from, how can anyone think of creating and supplying a product? How do we make the rest of a commodity stand out?

All those questions are answered by a creative mind. Creativity makes one think about how current business processes can be improved. A brand may be very established and famous with customers, but there is always something that can be achieved in a better way and different from them. The most unlikely ideas will come up with ingenuity and introduce innovation into current activities.

Creativity is merely the capacity to visualize. Imagination allows someone to enter places never previously explored. In business terms, creativity alone is what "thinking outside the box" is known as. Using creativity, an entrepreneur can set realistic expectations aside and dream about something inventive and imaginative.

However, in order to bring such innovative ideas to life in a business setting, a creative mind needs to have entrepreneurial skills. By evaluating available vs. necessary capital, how to set up a new company, and how to handle it, an entrepreneur examines the criteria of how to incorporate an idea. An entrepreneur creates business models that, in the first place, will help and implement creative ideas. An entrepreneur offers the 'scientific' element of how to bring to life creative imagination. An entrepreneur, therefore, crosses the gap between a creative genius and a conventional approach to business.

There are markers that signify a good entrepreneur's innovative thinking.

Creativity offers a competitive advantage to an entrepreneur, but how does one determine whether or not they are sufficiently creative?

Characteristic characteristics showing a talented entrepreneur are as follows:
- Only when they add value to the company and have the ability to draw more clients should an entrepreneur stick to rules and standards.
- As the first step, an entrepreneur plays with his ideas. The second step is to learn from experience, and the third step is to incorporate what they have learned.
- An entrepreneur is less fearful of failing and is still willing to pursue new projects.
- The Entrepreneur is not afraid of innovation and thinks that new ideas can only benefit their business.

- In any area that is directly or indirectly linked to a corporation, a creative thinker can take inspiration from new ideas.
- An entrepreneur has no fear of going outside the sector and entering new markets. This opens up a wide range of opportunities for new niches to be created.
- Every item and service is not sufficiently good and has room for improvement. An entrepreneur knows that very well.
- To produce new goods or services, an innovative thinker is involved in putting together completely opposite things.
- New products applicable to existing services and new services applicable to existing products are developed by an entrepreneur.
- Creative ideas come more easily because, regardless of who comes up with them, someone is not afraid to appreciate new ideas.
- An entrepreneur has an idea that he shares and is available to criticism that strengthens and refines the concept.
- Creativity arises from knowing various things, whether or not they are linked to the business.
- Such metrics illustrate that entrepreneurship and imagination go hand in hand with each other. Entrepreneurs are more agile, and more than they seek perfection, they seek to change.

Creativity must be coordinated.

Creativity requires a bit of structure for efficient implementation, despite all the versatility to pursue new projects. Too much structure, however, robs the entire essence of the process. Without being too strict, the secret lies in providing a rigorous approach to work. Researchers claim that with two different approaches: convergent and divergent, innovation works best. Using available knowledge, a convergent approach is based and finds a single solution. Divergent thought, however, works to produce several new concepts in various directions.

For entrepreneurship, innovative thinking is not the only ability required.

The debate so far has led us to conclude that entrepreneurship is profoundly rooted in certain essential skills: developing innovative ideas and having the courage to carry them out at risk. One should note, however, that this is not the only ability required for the effective implementation of an idea. It might be simple to generate an idea; it might be a difficult challenge to implement it successfully. What makes a person a good entrepreneur? Why do certain individuals grasp the possibilities that exist around them and others do not? Are they distinct genetically? Or do they have a different way of coping with things?

These problems do not have definite solutions, but some fields where an entrepreneur may have some experience have been pointed out by researchers. They are:

Personal characteristics. In a number of ways, personal qualities support entrepreneurs. All the qualities that make an entrepreneur stand out and have the ability to handle ventures are optimism, vision, self-control, and possessing initiative, determination, tolerance, and resilience.

Interpersonal credentials. At many levels, an entrepreneur has to communicate with individuals. This demands that they have outstanding interpersonal abilities. In a very competitive business setting, communication, leadership, inspiration, personal relations, negotiating skills, and ethics are qualities that are a must-have.

Looking objectively. His own critic must be an entrepreneur. Different aspects of an idea should be closely studied so it can be refined before implementation. When an idea is objectively analyzed, a lot of potential time can be saved, and no one else can do it better than the Entrepreneur himself.

Practical abilities. At the stage of concept implementation and management of the company, these skills are needed. An entrepreneur must be able to formulate objectives and activities and arrange them. Efficient decision-making and critical control at different stages of the process should take place.

The company thought vs. revolutionary thinking: what comes first?

This question is similar to which chicken or egg came first? The debate includes the factor the Entrepreneur first chooses to handle: the process's imaginative or realistic side.

Some assume that imagination is the initial stage of the process and the creation of the model for its implementation follows it. It may not always be accurate, however. Both of these processes are so intertwined with each other that their boundaries are very difficult to mark. From start to finish, both elements go hand in hand with each other. Creativity, however, could be dominant at the preliminary level, and during implementation, business thought could be at the helm or vice versa.

Fundamental elements of the creative process

Inherently complex and flexible is the method of producing fascinating projects. The method and the processes of the creative process have many facets. Below, some insight into the process is provided:

Stage 1: Planning and Preparation

Of course, the first stage is the preparation of some simple ideas to hold on to. There must be some inspiration that the entrepreneur "forces" or "prepares" to move forward. The creative process begins with an issue being identified and then investigated for relevant knowledge. This is done in an attempt to start searching for a solution that is feasible. To solve the problem, an entrepreneur looks in any direction, whether inside the industry or outside.

Phase 2: Outside the box thinking, moving outside the comfort zone

If we are not able to go outside our comfort zone, will we do anything? The safe arena must be left, go beyond, and take a chance. With attempts, incentives come.

'Thinking beyond the box' is a term that has been used since the 1970s in marketing, industry, and psychology. It owes its roots to a "nine-dot" game once used as a creativity exercise. The puzzle was constructed so that to find the solution, and the person had to go beyond the dots. Psychologists believe, however, that this "external" component is not necessarily external; it is merely the problem's current solution. "External" is just how it appears to be seen by our brain.

Step 3: Magic is not innovation.

It is certainly not magical, considering the immensely impressive things imagination can accomplish. Creativity is about seeing stuff from a different viewpoint. Copying various elements, transforming them, integrating them, and eureka can be the easiest approach to innovative thought! A new idea is there. This makes use of existing elements in essence. As Kirby Ferguson notes, "It occurs by applying to existing materials ordinary instruments of thought." And the soil that our creations evolve from is something that we despise and misinterpret, even though it gives us so much, and that's copying.

Stage 4: Incubation

Ideas that have the ability to solve a problem appear to thrive during the incubation period. The unconscious thinking process of refining an idea characterizes this point. Apparently, during this point, there are several operations at work, but the ultimate objective is to find a solution. In order to generate viable ideas, analyzing existing projects will help. Some scholars often refer to the process of innovation as re-creativity, as it draws inspiration from existing ideas and innovatively forms them.

Phase 5: Enlightenment

Incubation contributes to the clarification of thoughts. "This is the stage of "solution searching." Now the process of imagination leads to the realization of certain realistic ideas which can be put to use. It is like the moment of a "light bulb," so it's called illumination.

Phase 6: Testing

This stage decides whether or not the solution "found" still has the potential to function. The definition can either be approved as such, changed with minor or significant modifications, or fully rejected, causing the entire process to be done again.

Stage 7: Thought objectively

A comparatively, simple job is to produce new ideas. An entrepreneurial endeavor's main success lies in objectively evaluating the feasibility of a concept. In order to analyze the idea, logical thinking helps an entrepreneur to self-judge. It is characterized as a process of evaluating an idea that is self-directed, self-disciplined, self-monitored, and self-corrective.

Critical thinking provides the Entrepreneur with many strategic benefits, such as:
- It helps formulate the best idea possible.
- It allows for reaching new horizons and seeing the larger picture.
- It encourages the Entrepreneur to analyze and pose questions that were not previously considered.
- It helps to take decisive action; imagination results.

"Therefore, in the critical analysis of the viability of the idea, the process of creative thinking that begins with brainstorming "ends. The resulting potentially viable ideas will contribute to the development or enhancement of the existing ones of actual entrepreneurial enterprises.

No one else, like the Entrepreneur, is aware of the facets of the issue as well as the suggested solution. Therefore, a very honest opinion will come from the Entrepreneur himself about the feasibility of the project.

Entrepreneurship

Chapter 4: 7 Powerful Secrets of Thinking like an Entrepreneure

Successful entrepreneurs have something special — they have a way of thinking and behaving that is distinct from most people. The good news is that everyone, no matter what they do, can learn to think like an entrepreneur and to put these powerful secrets to use in their own lives.

1. Select Your Mindset

You are the one who, in your life, determines the behaviors and assumptions that you will take with you, and you are the one who can change them. If your mindset — and the work that you do — don't take you where you want to go, then change it. When you know you want more, refuse to actually settle for life and circumstances as they are.

2. Determination be rendered

Being determined is not only possessing the courage, strength, and persistence to move forward against the odds, but it is also being prepared for the battle strategically. You are placed in your decisions to be firm when you are committed, and you are ready to do the hard work needed to excel in everything you do. As venture capitalist Paul Graham pointed out, "The most important quality in an entrepreneur [is] not intelligence but determination."

3. Build a good bridge for relationships

Business is all about relationships, and in both business and life, creating good relationships is a road to success. Says Taulbert, "The ability to build strong relationships is crucial for survival and growth. Successful entrepreneurs are adept at building relationships." And over the long term, they are skilled at sustaining and developing them.

4. Slow down in order to lead

Business moves faster than ever, but great leadership means slowing down and having time to reflect on doing the things that are most important to your success. In particular, it means understanding and valuing the individuals you will meet in your company and personal life and taking them on your journey with you. Much like they can learn a lot from you, you have a lot to learn from them. As Richard Branson put it, "Other people have ideas also."

5. Know the company metrics for "health."

This image is not true at all, despite the common image of the entrepreneur who accomplishes great things simply by the power of their charisma or who wins flying by the seat of their pants. The most effective business people know exactly what makes their companies tick, and when appropriate, they keep a very close eye on the metrics — making quick fixes.

6. Be ready for upstream swimming

No one ever said that it was going to be easy to find success in business and life, and, honestly, it's not. Moments can occur when you can go with the tide, but you will always find that you have to swim upstream to make amazing things happen — against the current. Not only that, but several times in your life, you will have to change direction — changing tactics, careers, and even lives. Never stop; keep fighting. As Nelson Mandela said, "It always seems impossible until it's done."

7. Resolve to be efficient

Know that you can (you can!) achieve and then put all your energy into it. Once we are resolved — truly resolved — to do something, then nothing will deter us. Understand this secret, and the success you seek will be found.

4.1 12 Characteristics of the World's Most Successful Entrepreneurs

Here are 12 of the most common features I've seen with many of the most popular entrepreneurs in the world;

1. Total clarity of intent

Without exception, they are absolutely transparent as to why they are here and why their big picture exists. Some have the intention of making money (a lot of money), and others are here to use their power to change the world. This varies between them. There is no judgment on the actual intent here, but it is not possible to understate the significance of understanding their purpose.

2. They completely believe in themselves.

This is a fascinating trait. Each and every one of the world-class entrepreneurs I've worked with has an amazing sense of self-confidence once again. They absolutely back themselves up, even though no one else can. This is the hardest of all characteristics for me because it implies overcoming problems of doubt, anxiety, self-worth, and self-esteem and moving against the tribe, something that is very difficult to do on a strictly biological level for most of us.

3. They are really good at recognizing criteria and niches.

I sometimes think there are a pair of 'opportunity glasses' for successful entrepreneurs. In just about any case, they somehow seem able to find openings. This potential appears to be in niches, and the riches are in niches, as the old saying goes. When they find a niche, people in that niche are even better at solving problems.

4. Ability to concentrate first on the most significant items

The excellent book called "Focal Point" was written by Brian Tracy, in which he describes his method of concentrating and keeping focused. I assume that among successful entrepreneurs, this trait exists. They have the ability to monitor their thoughts and actions and to be fully present and centered on what is (and important) in front of them at the moment.

5. A Cultural Contribution

Both of these leaders have an amazingly compassionate disposition. It's what we call a culture of participation, and it's their way of leaving a legacy, making a difference, sharing their achievements, and much more. It is their purpose for many to be, but I prefer to think it has always been, but now they have the tools to do it.

6. An open-minded mind

To me, the oldest and the youngest are the most remarkable of these world-class entrepreneurs. The oldest has done stuff well beyond what most people could think of, but they still have an open mind. Instead, they are constantly searching for opportunities to learn more about what they do and, most importantly, how they can do it better. They don't rest on their laurels.

7. Incredible networks that they encourage and invest in,

These entrepreneurs obviously have amazing networks, but it is important to notice their attitude towards their network in speaking to them. They treat their networks with exemplary regard, without exception. Over many years, they have built up these partnerships, their connections in many ways are highly influential, and they have the potential to expand each other's company in leaps and bounds. They spend time and energy in their networks, give more than they take, and behave without reciprocating expectations.

8. Investing in yourself at all stages

Elite entrepreneurs recognize that they need to improve their talents, take physical and mental care of themselves, and take time to recharge their batteries on a regular basis. This is a necessary activity, not an optional activity.

9. They challenge themselves constantly,

In this entrepreneurial community, I definitely see this trait - they challenge themselves all the time, in every way possible. They're major learners, they're doing things that leave their comfort zones, they're physically pushing themselves, they're working hard, and they're playing hard. They are made solid by this mentality that facilitates self-challenge. This makes them more capable of dealing with the challenges of life that we all face. It keeps their minds active, suits their bodies, and optimistic about their attitudes.

10. They believe in machines.

Interestingly enough, many of these amazing entrepreneurs are Neanderthals of techno, but that doesn't stop them from believing in the merit of it. Nor does it deter them from spending massive quantities of money on software to do what they do better. It is the conviction that is more meaningful than their own individual abilities. They can pursue it as new technology becomes available, invest in it to see if it can make their business and their lives more aligned with what they want to accomplish.

11. Build resilience

In our lives, we all face ups and downs. Some unfortunate individuals have a nearly infinite supply of downs that most of us will break. In their lives, all of the high-achieving entrepreneurs I have observed have had immense struggles. They could have hidden behind these difficulties easily and played the victim, but they didn't. Over time, they have been resilient, and every day they get more resilient.

12. A Mentality Millionaire

With the right mentality, the difference between a rich entrepreneur and a poor entrepreneur is always one that accepts abundance and opportunity. I see so many people struggling in the industry; they always have and always will, simply because they have to break down their financial home base. It is important for everyone trapped in this area to start reprogramming their brain. It is possible to change any narrow belief; we just need to have a powerful enough motivation to change. Build your own millionaire mind if you are sick of being broke.

Conclusion

The development or extraction of value is entrepreneurship. With this concept, entrepreneurship is seen as change, typically involving risk beyond what is usually experienced in starting a company, which may involve values other than merely economic ones.

More limited definitions have identified entrepreneurship as the process of creating, launching, and running a new company, often initially a small business, or as the' capacity and willingness to grow, organize and manage a business venture along with any of its risks to make a profit. Entrepreneurs are often referred to as the people who build these businesses. Though definitively specified

The word entrepreneur is used in the field of economics for an individual capable of turning innovations or technologies into goods and services.

In this context, entrepreneurship defines operations on the part of both existing companies and new enterprises.

References

Neil Patel. n.d. *30 Ways To Become A More Successful Entrepreneur*. [online] Available at: <https://neilpatel.com/blog/become-successful-entrepreneur/>.

Global Entrepreneurship Institute. n.d. *Understanding Entrepreneurship*. [online] Available at: <https://news.gcase.org/understanding-entrepreneurship/#:~:text=Entrepreneurship%20begins%20with%20an%20idea,also%20means%20taking%20on%20risks.>.

What is Enterpreneurship | Everything About Entrepreneurship. n.d. *Things Entrepreneurs Should Know Before Starting A Business*. [online] Available at: <https://101entrepreneurship.org/things-entrepreneurs-should-know-before-starting-a-business/>.

Inc.com. n.d. *7 Powerful Secrets Of Thinking Like An Entrepreneur*. [online] Available at: <https://www.inc.com/peter-economy/7-powerful-secrets-of-thinking-like-an-entrepreneur.html>.

www.ingramcontent.com/pod-product-compliance
Lightning Source LLC
Chambersburg PA
CBHW080611220526
45466CB00010B/3314